The 24-7 Prayer Manual

survivor

ISBN 1 84291 162 7

Published by
KINGSWAY COMMUNICATIONS LTD
Lottbridge Drove, Eastbourne BN23 6NT, England.
Email: books@kingsway.co.uk

Book design and production for the publishers by
Bookprint Creative Services, P.O. Box 827, BN21 3YJ, England.
Printed in Great Britain.

'24–7 is brilliant. If you're wanting to combine social involvement with spiritual intimacy, this is an absolutely fantastic tool!' (*Steve Chalke – Founder, Oasis Trust and TV presenter*)

'24–7 is making history as an unstoppable global prayer movement, and has caught the imagination of a rising generation, involving many tens of thousands in urgent, persistent, continuous, world-changing intercession, encouraging radical discipleship and effective mission. This brilliant book will inspire you with practical help on how to establish 24–7 in your own community.' (*Dr Patrick Dixon – Director, Global Change Ltd and author of* Futurewise)

'The 24–7 prayer movement is one of the most out-of-control God things anywhere on the planet at the moment. Whatever you do, don't just read about it – Catch the Fire!' (*Andy Hawthorne – Director, The Message Trust*)

'This has to be one of the most exciting movements in the church today. I'm excited about what 24–7 is teaching, and I'm eager to learn more from this book myself.' (*Rob Frost – Director, Share Jesus International*)

'God's mission to save lost humanity is the central theme of Scripture. Jesus Christ is the key to it all. All of our discipleship, worship and prayer is part of this great mission. The heart of 24–7 is to bring prayer and mission together and do this in a way which flows out of the instincts and culture of the emerging generations. I've been in and around 24–7 since it started. Run by a bunch of nobodies, surfing the waves of the Spirit and making it up as they went along. The rest is history. Check out the story and get involved. Let's see where the waves will take us!' (*Roger Ellis – Director, Fusion and leader of Revelation Church*)

'24–7 was a God-idea that has swept around the globe. Prayer has always preceded revivals, the re-evangelisation of people groups and the transformation of society. Throw yourself into the river of prayer; it could be the best thing you have ever done. (*Gerald Coates, Team Leader, Pioneer, author, broadcaster*)

'It is so important we come together to pray at such a time as this. 24–7 seems well positioned to do just that.' (*George Carey, former Archbishop of Canterbury*)

'I think 24–7 prayer is one of the greatest things we have experienced in recent years and we will never be the same again.' (*Commissioner Alex Hughes, Territorial Commander, Salvation Army, UK*)

'It is absolutely thrilling to witness thousands of young people discovering the power of prayer through the 24–7 movement. I believe the key to reaching our world is passion, prayer, practical action and proclamation, and 24–7 combines all four! I wholeheartedly commend 24–7 to churches, universities and all those longing for the coming of God's Kingdom.' (*Lyndon Bowring*)

'24–7 is about prayer – a lifeline to our creator God. It helps us to stand in the gap and intercede for the things we're passionate about, to see things happen and to witness miracles!' (*Andy Hunter, DJ and recording artist*)

For Jesus,
the author and perfecter
of every prayer . . .

With thanks to the 24–7 crew around the world. This book has evolved from our relationships and discoveries together over three years as we have sought to surf this wave together. Thanks also to Dave Roberts and the team at Kingsway, to the Revd Matt Rees for his research at the Bodleian library in Oxford and to Phil Baldwin, a non-Christian named on the wall of the first prayer room, who now holds this movement together.

Contents

Introduction

'(Jesus) always lives to intercede . . .' (Hebrews 7:25)

Jesus himself lives to intercede and so can we. But prayer is perhaps the area in which we most spectacularly fail to practise what we preach. Most of us rarely do it and we know we should. 24–7 is a practical tool helping us all to live up to our aspirations in prayer. It is both a model and a movement, helping ordinary people to mirror Jesus by praying persistently, living to intercede. With this book any church anywhere can learn to pray like never before.

Throughout history, the tide has turned through movements and moments of continual prayer. From the Upper Room of Pentecost, ancient Celtic monasteries and papal edicts, via the incredible eighteenth-century Moravian hundred-year prayer meeting and the outrageously inter-racial prayer room of Azusa Street in Los

Angeles, right up to the modern-day 24–7 phenomenon, continual prayer has marked some of the church's
most astonishing moments.

'The vision behind 24-7 is
directly from heaven. It
just works!'
(Ocke Kruger - Germany)

This book includes everything you need to know to:

- mobilise continual intercession in your community
  without burning out
- organise a life-changing prayer room full of creativity
  where you live
- join a prayer meeting that's continued without a
  moment's break since 1999

As young people desert church and the AIDS pandemic
orphans Africa, there can be little doubt that God is calling his people to pray and obey as never before. But:

- How should we practically respond?
- What does prayer look like in a postmodern world?
- How do we get young people excited about inter-
  cession?
- How do we encourage creativity, discipline and inti-
  macy in personal prayer?
- How do we avoid intercession becoming a specialist
  activity for a distinct few?

- How do we keep our prayers earthed and effective in the real world?

This book seeks to answer all these questions by equipping you to run a non-stop prayer meeting where you live, putting prayer back at the very heart of your community.

To make the book user-friendly, it is divided into three sections, each one broken down into five bite-size chunks:

SECTION 1: the first five chapters introduce the concept of 24–7 prayer and how we stumbled upon it.
SECTION 2: five easy steps walking you through all the practicalities of running a prayer room.
SECTION 3: five helpful keys, unpacking the thinking behind 24–7, for those wanting to go a bit deeper.

24–7 works because it's a network of people sharing resources and experiences all round the world. If you register your prayer room with our website you can get loads of really useful prayer resources, plus access to a special 1:1 helpline for prayer room organisers. The 24–7 network is here to help you in any way we can to have a life-changing experience of prayer. So, please relax!

Thousands of people have already discovered that 24–7 prayer works in dozens of nations, most denominations and in locations as diverse as the US Naval Academy, an English cathedral, a German punk festival, a Swiss skate park and a South African school. And if all these people in all these places can do it, so can you!

'I have posted watchmen on your walls, O Jerusalem; they will never be silent day or night. You who call on the LORD, give yourselves no rest, and give him no rest till he establishes Jerusalem and makes her the praise of the earth.'
(Isaiah 62:6-7)

SECTION 1:

DISCOVERING
24-7 PRAYER
(THE MOTIVATIONAL BIT)

Chapter 1: Déjà vu
- AN ACCIDENT PLANNED BY GOD

Stepping into the room he gasped. It was all there: the globe, the candle, the walls and floor, even the ceiling covered in spidery writing and childish paintings.

A good-looking guy in training kit sat by a lava lamp, hunch-slumped in a beanbag reading his Bible. In the corner there was a student kneeling and praying so quietly that her whispers sounded like a single rustling leaf. A younger girl had identified her school on a large local map papered across one wall and was writing something on it. A chart by the door was covered with names of those signed up to spend shifts in this unusual environment.

And now, standing in this room, Nick gasped with recognition. 'I've been here before,' he whispered, shaking his head. 'It was last year and God gave me a vision of people praying in a room like this. There was a candle,' he recalled, indicating the one in the middle of the room, 'and a globe. And it always seemed strange because there was graffiti all over the walls and the floor and the ceiling. That's why I remember it. I could never understand the writing. And now I'm here, standing in the middle of my vision. I just walked into the room I saw last year.'

In those early, explosive weeks of our first prayer room, in Chichester on the south coast of England, discoveries like Nick's pre-emptive vision were almost daily occurrences. We quickly realised that our big idea of trying to pray non-stop for a month had in fact been God's much bigger idea in the first place.

Unseen voices

A young mum on a night vigil heard someone else praying in the room. She searched the place, all the while hearing the tones of that other visitor, but finding herself alone she came to the startling conclusion that an unseen angel was quietly accompanying her prayers. You can imagine the buzz as stories like that spread. There was a corporate spine-tingle among those hungry for God's presence (and such a longing is not the exclusive domain of churchgoers).

> 'There was a corporate spine-tingle among those hungry for God's presence'

Before long a book of stories and answered prayers began to fill up with testimonies to the power of prayer. Meanwhile there were other prayers that remained unanswered – agonising heart-cries posted on our 'Wailing Wall' for dying relatives and unbelieving friends, expressing unbearable personal pain. It was incredible to see the wounds of a community literally mapped out on a wall like that, and it meant that we could actually carry one another's burdens in a way that no big meeting can. Of course we were also celebrating one another's breakthroughs and insights in prayer. It was both exciting and agonising to be in that room as part of a community praying like never before.

The Vision

A long poem written on the wall of that first prayer room somehow took on a life of its own. Someone must have copied it down and emailed it to someone else because within weeks The Vision (as it became known) was circulating the underground church in China, being published in America and even choreographed in Spain! We just kept shaking our heads in amazement.

God in the house

But looking back on those days, the most wonderful thing of all about that first prayer room was not the art, the honesty or the sheer, startling fact that a church so bad at prayer suddenly found itself interceding every minute of the day and night. The most wonderful thing about that room was that God was there. There was a pervasive awareness of his presence, rumours of eternity and a certain spiritual momentum generated by many hours of unbroken prayer.

We began to realise that the Holy Spirit can fill a place as well as a person. The ancient Celts used to describe such locations as 'thin places', where the veil between heaven and earth becomes so fine that prayer is easier and the still, small voice is more clearly heard.

'one hour in the prayer room felt like ten minutes'

Time and time again people said that one hour in the prayer room felt like ten minutes. And this was from people whose previous experience had been the exact opposite: ten minutes of prayer often feeling more like an hour!

Atheist antennae

Even non-Christians could sense the Lord's presence in that room, whispering, 'Wow – you can really feel God in here!' On one occasion the visitor was reminded that he didn't actually believe in God, but replied without hesitation, 'Yeah, I don't. But you can really *feel* him in here, can't you?'

We were beginning to discover that people who don't want to be preached at still want to be prayed for. People who don't think they believe in God still believe in prayer. And some people who don't so much as go to church actually don't mind rolling up at a prayer room – even in the middle of the night!

Our experience of God in the prayer room was both mystical and practical. On the walls there was always so much to see: messages that could move the hardest heart, children's pictures, intimate prayer requests, poems of worship, graffiti'd Bible verses, prophetic symbols and, of course, that evolving book of answered prayer. For many people, visiting that room to see such things and meet with God became a mini-pilgrimage, especially at three in the morning on a cold winter's night.

How it works

Prayer rooms seem to provide a focus and a framework that many of us need in living up to our aspirations in prayer. Of course, 'accountability' and 'discipline' aren't exactly the most thrilling words in the dictionary, but they are vital to discipleship. So the prayer room's system of shifts in a fixed location undoubtedly helps us to pray, because if we don't turn up to do a slot, it will be noticed! This can be a helpful incentive, sometimes dragging us screaming and kicking into God's presence!

For most people 24–7 works something like this:

> On Sunday at church you get fired up and decide to give God an hour or two of exclusive time in the week ahead.
>
> In that flush of rash enthusiasm, you find yourself

signing up on the 24–7 rota to visit the prayer room at 3 o'clock Tuesday morning.

This means that two days later, a demonised alarm clock rips you from your bed on a cold winter's night that's already much too short, sandwiched wafer-thin between busy days. Resisting the urge to hit the 'snooze' button for the fourth time, you stagger semi-comatose from bed, haunted by the memory of Sunday's foolish prayer pledge, and hating the fact that some poor soul on the other side of town can't leave the prayer room until you turn up to relieve them!

When you arrive at the room, the previous person passes on the baton in prayer and goes home to bed.

And that's often the defining moment: the click of the door as the previous person leaves. It's the moment you find yourself alone in a room with God in the middle of the night; the moment you discover the reality of God's promise to be found by those who truly seek him with all their hearts (Jeremiah 29:13). At this moment all the talk about prayer, the guilt at your prayerlessness, the theory, the apathy, the hectic schedule, evaporates. It's now or never. You and God, face to face, looking for words in the silence. In a complicated world, this is the simple, inevitable core. Many 24–7 regulars still consider themselves bad at praying, yet they find a single hour in the prayer room insufficient, and sign up for two.

When you look at the facts of what happened next, and the way that a solitary prayer room became a thousand by accident, the only rational explanation is that God turned up and has continued to turn up in prayer rooms ever since.

'"Then you will call upon me and come and pray to me, and I will listen to you. You will seek me and find me when you seek me with all your heart. I will be found by you," declares the LORD.'
(Jeremiah 29:12-14)

Chapter 2: Critical mass
- A PRAYER ROOM EXPLODES

'May I know Thee more
clearly
Love Thee more dearly
And follow Thee more
nearly.'
(St Richard of Chichester,
1197-1253)

It happened by accident. It was never planned, strat-egised, studied, budgeted or even expected, but that prayer room just began to multiply.

At the end of our first month of continual prayer we were unable to stop – the momentum was too great; too many people were still wanting to spend time alone in that room with God.

After a second month the momentum was, if any-thing, even greater. And then in November 1999 our lit-tle prayer room in the shadow of Chichester Cathedral began to spontaneously self-seed around the world as word spread and the idea caught on.

Other groups began to email us, saying that they'd heard about what we were doing and had decided to do the same, praying non-stop in a room for a week or more. A five-minute notice at a conference called Cultural Shift inspired 34 youth churches to do the same. We began to wonder if it might somehow be possible to fill an entire year with non-stop prayer by linking all these emerging prayer rooms together. A church of a hundred adults in Sidcup near London went away and prayed for 15 weeks without a break. To help such people we hurriedly scribbled resources on scraps of paper (one of which gave rise to this book!) and for the sake of convenience (without much imagination) christened this accidental proliferation '24–7 prayer'.

> 'At the time of writing there have been many hundreds of 24–7 prayer rooms in 46 nations'

To our amazement, God hired us a brilliant web designer called Pete Worthington to link up all the prayer rooms in cyberspace. Pete is one of the nicest guys you could hope to meet and has been working for 24–7 unpaid ever since! The site he designed on a scrap of paper at Pete and Samie Greig's kitchen table now gets more than a million hits every month, and has been translated into various languages and cultures.

At the time of writing there have been many hundreds of 24–7 prayer rooms in 46 nations, in most denominations and in locations as diverse as a German Bible school, an American Ivy League college and a police station near London.

24–7–365

We have also been able to help networks such as Youth With A Mission, Pioneer and the Salvation Army give themselves to years of unbroken prayer in various countries. One Salvation Army officer had tears in his eyes as he described their year of prayer as the most significant development he could recall in 50 years of ministry. Some citadels had seen their first conversions in years and even William Booth had never thought of doing this! When the Swedish Free Churches completed an unbroken year of prayer at the stroke of midnight on 31st December 2002, they knew they'd achieved something genuinely historic in their nation's history, unprecedented since the time of the Vikings.

New order

As well as facilitating such years of prayer, 24–7 has launched a few prayer houses (we call them boiler rooms). These are modelled on the ancient Celtic *muintir*, or monasteries, and are lay communities based in urban centres that serve as prayer houses but also mission centres, art studios and pilgrims' hostels.

Alongside these boiler rooms, and as a natural extension of so many prayer rooms, we have been able to mobilise mission teams, targeting the 'high places of youth culture'. We always aim to catalyse and support church planting, working with existing churches to do so wherever we can. In prayer rooms a number of people have already received long-term calls to other nations. 24–7 mission teams are travelling all over the world, seeking to 'pray, play and obey' in locations as diverse as the mountains of Mexico, the slums of Delhi and the biggest nightclubs in the world on the Mediterranean island of Ibiza.

Looking back, looking forward . . .

> 'Now to him who is able to do immeasurably more than all we ask or imagine . . . to him be the glory.'
> (Ephesians 3:20)

In just a few years, we have watched prayer rooms springing up spontaneously all over the world, mission teams being sent out and boiler rooms planted. It's been quite a ride! Again and again we've been left shaking our heads in amazement as God has done 'immeasurably more' than all we could possibly have asked or imagined.

But it's not really about all the big stuff. The heart of 24–7 is the teenager who is praying right now as you read this book. It's about the email we received this morning saying that another person just walked into a prayer room and met Jesus for the very first time. It's about the depressed mother, saved from suicide by the care of the 24–7 web community. It's about the student daring to ask his friend in the bar for a prayer request.

In reading this book, perhaps God is speaking to you about joining in with this chorus of prayer that has filled every minute of every day since its accidental instigation in 1999.

Three old ladies (and an occasional dog)

> 'Blessed are the poor in spirit, for theirs is the kingdom of heaven.'
> (Matthew 5:3)

The danger of telling this amazing story is that you may by now be boxing us as a bunch of super-saint prayer warriors, so it's very important to put some kind of context on the church where 24–7 began. We were and are an active and relational community with lots going on, but prior to 24–7, our weekly prayer meetings really only seemed to attract a handful of godly old ladies (and once a dog). The phrase 'half-night of prayer' was enough to strike fear into most hearts and the thing that made this prayer famine even more embarrassing was that a man with a proven prophetic ministry had once predicted that we would become a house of prayer for the nations. To be honest, most of us anticipated pigs flying to the moon long before we could ever live up to that particular prophetic word.

But no matter how convicted we felt about our prayerlessness, we knew that it wasn't enough simply to try harder. Striving wasn't going to be the answer. Guilt trips don't go anywhere. We needed God to break in and teach us, super-practically, how to pray. And so he did!

> 'Lord, teach us to
> pray . . .' (Luke 11:1)

Chapter 3: The Z factor
- THE 100-YEAR PRAYER MEETING

'Could you . . . not keep
watch with me for one
hour? . . .
Watch and pray so that
you will not fall into
temptation.'
(Matthew 26:40-41)

The year is 1727 and the summer sunshine is flooding through the windows of a country church near Dresden, Germany, where a community of refugees has gathered to share communion. The bread and the wine are especially meaningful to this particular group, who have known their fair share of bursting veins and broken bodies.

Just five years earlier they had fled for their lives across the Austrian Alps under fierce religious persecution, hounded by the Counter Reformation away from their homes and livelihoods. Leaving Moravia in search of a new beginning, this rag-tag mix of politically incorrect misfits had been granted permission to settle here in Saxony on the estate of a 22-year-old aristocrat called Count Nikolaus Von Zinzendorf. Here they hoped to build a truly Christian community, peacefully united around the Bible alone.

But five years later we find this New Jerusalem torn by small-minded discontent. The Moravian refugees have spent half a decade competing, disagreeing and dividing. The body is well and truly broken and Zinzendorf, now aged 27, has had enough.

That's why he's gathered them here today in the church at Bethelsdorf, insisting upon apologies all round. And now, finding themselves forced to reflect on the broken body on the cross and the broken body of their community, hard hearts are softening. One at a time people stand, some with tears running down their cheeks, to confess sinful attitudes and express forgiveness.

The watch of the Lord

And that was the moment it all began; the moment that would somehow rewrite the history books of the next three centuries. There, in that village church on 13th August 1727, the Spirit of God moved with such power in the repentant hearts of those Moravian dreamers that they began to pray like never before and continued without a break for more than a hundred years.

A moment of grace had given momentum to a

movement for change which would re-landscape much of the Western world right up to the present day. Tucked away in the immaculate village of Hernnhut, where modern-day Germany meets Poland and the Czech Republic, those Moravians quietly determined that the flame of God's presence should 'be kept burning on the altar continuously' without ever being allowed to go out (Leviticus 6:13). And so they organised themselves to keep the 'watch of the Lord', praying in one-hour shifts round the clock as the very heartbeat to their community.

> 'those Moravians quietly determined that the flame of God's presence should "be kept burning on the altar continuously"'

Widespread arson

As they maintained that flame of intercession, the fire of their own prayers consumed them. The Moravians soon found themselves burning with passion for those without Jesus, compelled by his Great Commission and his great compassion simply to go. And so in 1732, after five years of continuous prayer, Zinzendorf, the young leader of the Moravians at Hernnhut, quietly commissioned the first great missions thrust of the Reformation.

Moravians quickly spread out all over the known world, propelled by that incredible prayer meeting, preaching the gospel wherever they went, often at great personal cost. Two members of the community even volunteered to sell themselves into slavery so as to carry the gospel to the plantations of the West Indies. When an unknown clergyman named John Wesley was converted through the joyful witness of Moravian missionaries on a transatlantic ship in a storm, he headed off to Hernnhut straight away for discipleship from Zinzendorf.

Martin Luther had founded training institutions in an unfruitful attempt to turn his Reformation into world mission, but it was Zinzendorf's 24–7 prayer meeting in a rural backwater that had become a springboard for the greatest missionary movement of his generation. In the ensuing 200 years, 3,000 missionaries were shot out like rockets to the very ends of the earth. The flame of prayer on that unlikely altar could not be contained by geographical or doctrinal boundaries. The flame became wildfire.

Stepping up to the plate

Some 300 years later, in an equally unlikely place (Chichester, on the south coast of England), we knew that God was calling us to prayer, but that we were bad at it. Remembering the Moravians we began to wonder if there was something powerful in their non-stop model that had unleashed so much passion. Visiting Hernnhut, Pete Greig concluded that if they could pray for a hundred years then we could surely do a mere month in one-hour shifts back in England.

It seemed like a really good idea until we worked out how many hours there are in a month. But then again, there was an excitement about the idea; a stirring in our hearts and a sneaking suspicion that for some perverse reason young people were more likely to turn up to pray at three in the morning than at seven-thirty on a Thursday evening. And anyway, if we only managed a week, we figured it would still be a lot more praying than most of us had done in years! We weren't trying to get into the *Guinness Book of Records*. We were just hoping to learn to pray.

Some people cautioned us to build up to such an extreme season gradually, but we knew that without an extreme challenge and strict discipline we would simply end up with a series of poorly attended prayer meetings, destined to decline dismally in a whimper of self-condemnation.

Ask . . . seek . . . knock

> 'Ask and you'll get;
> Seek and you'll find;
> Knock and the door will
> open.'
> (Luke 11:9, THE MESSAGE)

And so, on 5th September 1999, we gathered the youth congregation of Revelation Church, taught about the Moravians, lit a candle and began talking with God. The first few hours were really difficult as we adhered to the conventional prayer meeting model, all gathered in an empty hall trying to think of things to say out loud.

Secretly a few of us began to wonder if this whole idea had been a big mistake. But at midnight we moved into the prayer room, which had been decorated beautifully to inspire us, with different areas cleverly shaped from tents and sheets. And as we began to take shifts alone in that room, we began to discover why Jesus had so often sought solitude to pray. In seeking God we were finding him, in asking we were receiving and in knocking on the wooden door of that first prayer room tucked away on an industrial estate in southern England, we were finding ourselves welcomed into the very presence of God.

> 'Go into your room, close
> the door and pray to your
> Father, who is unseen.'
> (Matthew 6:6)

Chapter 4: 24-7 prayer through the ages
- THE HISTORY AND MYSTERY OF CONTINUAL PRAYER

'We need space and time to contemplate and meditate. In fact, time to stop is becoming a rare commodity. . . . We can counter the culture by promoting the idea of sacred space. We can give people the time, the peace, the quiet and the reflection that they just don't get outside - the time for prayer and worship; the time to think about the things that really count.'[1]

As 24–7 snowballed into other nations we turned to Scripture and church history, hoping to make sense of what was happening. As we did so, it quickly became clear that the concept of 24–7 prayer was not new, and it certainly hadn't been invented by the Moravians. With mounting excitement we discovered that, throughout history, God has raised up communities like ours, committed to the *laus perennis* (continual praise and prayer), especially at times of spiritual and social crisis. These prayer movements have sometimes been the very calling card of revival and transformation.

> 'throughout history, God has raised up communities like ours, committed to the *laus perennis*'

Somehow, it seemed, we had stumbled upon a strategic key to spiritual influence, largely neglected in our time yet deployed consistently by our forefathers. We felt like a bunch of kids at the seaside, suddenly caught up in a wave so big we knew it could crush us.

Remixing history

The history of 24–7 prayer down the ages is rich, full of surprising characters and occasionally even funny! In this chapter there is only space for a whirlwind tour, but a fuller account can be found in another 24–7 title, *Red Moon Rising*, which tells our story in much more detail.

In the beginning

In the beginning was relationship: uninterrupted intimacy between Adam and Eve and God. The whole earth was, in effect, a prayer room: a place of wonder and interaction between creation and Creator. Each day, in the cool of the evening, that unbroken fellowship would focus in upon a walk with God through the glades of Eden. It was a time, even in paradise, of deliberate and delightful prayer.

The tabernacle

This picture of unbroken intimacy with God recurs like the frames of a film, strobing from Genesis to Revelation. Again and again, God seeks out people with whom he can walk and talk in daily communion, just as he did in the Garden of Eden. He calls Abraham 'my friend' (Isaiah 41:8) and converses with Moses 'face to face, as a man speaks with his friend' (Exodus 33:11). These intimate conversations would take place in 'the tent of meeting' or tabernacle – a mobile prayer room, hosting God's presence at the very heart of the community.

The tabernacle was so important to the Israelites that nearly one-third of the book of Exodus is devoted to it. As they camped at Sinai they spent many months and vast amounts of their treasure and endeavour constructing this stunning, symbolic prayer room to travel with them wherever they went. It was a defining moment. The tabernacle marked the fact that, through revelation and rescue, Yahweh had become the very essence of their national identity and hope. His presence belonged at the very heart of their community night and day.

> 'His presence belonged at the very heart of their community night and day.'

The Hebrew sense of history, destiny and community all now centred on the presence of God in their midst, 24 hours a day and seven days a week.

> 'The tabernacle . . . pointed to the chief end of man: to glorify God and to enjoy him forever. Above every other consideration was the fact that the omnipotent, unchanging and transcendent God of all the universe had, by means of the tabernacle, graciously come to "dwell" or "tabernacle" with his people.'
> (EXPOSITORY BIBLE COMMENTARY)

The tabernacle was an astounding symbol of the presence of God, but it was far more than this. This tent was not just an ancient, nomadic equivalent of the locked church building on a contemporary village green. The tabernacle was a place alive with relationship, interaction, guidance and prayer. It was above the tabernacle that the pillars of cloud and fire appeared, leading the people forward and telling them when to rest. The tabernacle really was the place of prayer as well as presence. Jack Hayford puts it like this: 'The tabernacle is not a great hall for the assembling of multitudes, but a place of personal encounter where worshippers may bring their covenant offerings.'[2]

The temple

As the people of Israel settled in the Promised Land, that tabernacle tent evolved into a great temple building, described by the prophet Isaiah as 'a house of prayer for all nations' (Isaiah 56:7; Matthew 21:13). The prayer room had become a prayer house, in which the priests worshipped continually in disciplined shifts for a thousand years, apart from the exile in Babylon.

> 'The priests kept watch throughout the night in the Temple, and slept on site.'[3]

This priestly service of perpetual praise and prayer was known as the *Tamid*, and particularly referred to three symbolic aspects of temple life:

● The morning and evening sacrifice

- The burning of incense (a symbol in both Testaments of prayer)
- The burning of the menorah candles and the fire on the golden altar

An exceptionally rare word is used to describe the candles and the fire on the altar: *anaposbestos*, which refers to inextinguishable, eternal, perpetual lights. Some 2,000 years later, this concept became an important one for our friends the Moravians as they sought to maintain the flame of intercession continually on the altar of their lives.

The human heart

Forty years before its physical destruction that glorious temple became spiritually redundant. A thousand years of perpetual prayer within its courts came to their bloody fulfilment as Jesus, who had come and 'tabernacled' among us (John 1:14), cried, 'It is finished!' and gave up his spirit. Matthew records how 'at that moment the curtain of the temple was torn in two from top to bottom. The earth shook and the rocks split. The tombs broke open and the bodies of many holy people who had died were raised to life' (27:51–52). This was the ultimate, spine-tingling 'amen' to the ceaseless prayers of the tabernacle and temple. In that moment the gates of Eden were flung open for anyone to come in without shame or fear, and to walk and talk once again with God in the cool of the evening.

And at that moment 24–7 prayer changed for ever. It was never again to be locked away in tents and temples for an exclusive, representative few. Instead, each one of us could become a walking talking prayer room, a temple for the Holy Spirit. From this moment onwards the only true 24–7 prayer room was going to be that of the human heart in which God is being worshipped and welcomed continually.

> 'The point was not with whom one prayed, nor where, nor in what form, nor at what fixed time . . . but that one's very life be totally prayer.'[4]

When we set aside particular places for 24–7 prayer, these can be outward expressions of perpetual inner prayerfulness as we host God's presence. Sometimes this hosting will be subconscious; for instance as we sleep or use our brains to think about lesser things. But to maintain this state of heart and mind, we must regularly move prayer from the subconscious to the conscious realm, deliberately inviting Christ out of the twilight and into the limelight of our lives. There are many ways of doing this: taking a regular walk outside, maintaining a daily 'quiet time', saying grace before each meal, wearing a 'What Would Jesus Do?' bracelet, keeping a journal, attending a weekly church meeting or maintaining a bedtime ritual. Every person is different, but we all need to find those people and places that enable us to re-centre on Christ regularly, so that the reflex reaction of our lives remains prayerful, all the time.

A season of 24–7 prayer provides a place, a time, a context and a catalyst for this conscious and persistent prayer to continue, both individually and as communities. The prayer room is a picture of something going on all the time in the heart of every believer. It helps us maintain the flame of worship upon the altar of our lives. We leave the prayer room encouraged and enabled to keep on praying consciously and subconsciously through the trials of the day ahead.

The Upper Room

Reeling from the events of the previous week, the disciples returned to Jerusalem, where 'they all joined together constantly in prayer' (Acts 1:14). Pentecost came to that prayer room and the rest, of course, is history. Thousands of people suddenly found that they could walk right into the presence of God whenever and wherever they wanted. The curtain had been torn in two, making the Holy of Holies accessible to ordinary people in ordinary places. As a result, prayer rooms began to spring up everywhere, with astonishing results. The disciples, we are told, devoted themselves to prayer (Acts 2:42) in one another's homes, Solomon's colonnade, in boats and even in gaol. The impact was so extraordinary that within a few years they could be accused of 'turning the world upside down' through their perseverance in prayer and in proclaiming the gospel.

> 'Be joyful always; pray continually.'
> (1 Thessalonians 5:16-17)

The early Church Fathers (first to third centuries)

As Christianity grew, 24–7 prayer was expressed in many ways. In the very first monasteries (founded by Pachomius), we know that there were all-night watches from dusk to dawn, normally as acts of private devotion rather than big communal nights of prayer. In AD 250, Cyprian challenged his fellow African Christians to 'be as vigilant at night as in the light of day', continuing: 'Let us not cease here (at night) also to pray and give thanks to God.'[5] There were similar seasons of night-and-day prayer throughout the first three centuries, mentioned in the writings of Athanasius of Alexandria and others.[6]

Alexander the Sleepless (b. 355)

One of the most colourful characters in the history of 24–7 prayer is Alexander the Sleepless. Alexander was born to wealthy parents on a Greek island and became a Christian while studying in Constantinople (now Istanbul). He immediately gave away all his possessions, moved to Syria and joined a monastery. But he got more and more frustrated, and after four years could bear it no longer. Approaching the abbot he asked, 'Are the things in the gospel really true?' When the abbot

> 'Alexander flew into a rage, grabbed his Bible and quit.'

assured him that the gospel was indeed trustworthy, Alexander challenged his superior: 'Then why do we not put them into practice?' When the abbot replied that 'no one can possibly observe them', Alexander flew into a rage, grabbed his Bible and quit.

He began to gather other radically minded monks, all of whom gave their possessions to the poor and committed themselves to live simply and prayerfully. So many gathered around Alexander that he was soon forced to divide them according to their language: Romans, Greeks, Syrians and Egyptians, to pray continually in shifts (hence the nickname 'sleepless').

Alexander's tribes prayed 24–7 wherever they went: camped in the desert and in busy cities while ministering to the poor. When they entered cities they would often be assaulted and expelled by the ecclesiastical powers, which felt intimidated by such a radical example. One scholar depicts the way that 'Alexander's troupe combined the charismatic dynamism of a mobile house of prayer with the potential menace of any well-organised, hundred-man gang. It would have been impossible to ignore their appearance on the urban scene!'[7] On one occasion Alexander's praying 'heavies' may even have prayed 24–7 on a boat sailing up and down the Euphrates river!

The Acoemetae (fifth to ninth centuries)

It was probably Alexander the Sleepless who founded the order of the Acoemetae in AD 400. A single 24–7 prayer community quickly grew into several massive monasteries in the Black Sea region and Constantinople, becoming renowned for generations for their learning as well as their perpetual prayer.

St Maurice (515 to present day)

The oldest place of continuous worship in the Western world is a monastery in the town of St Maurice in Switzerland. There, for one and a half millennia, lovers of Jesus have conducted the *laus perennis*, a source of blessing upon Switzerland and a centre of study and influence around the world.

St Maurice was a Roman commander of the Theban (North African) legion in the third century AD. Maximian Caesar sent him to quell an uprising in the Alps, but on arriving Maurice discovered that these rebels were all Coptic Christians like himself – his brothers in Christ. St Maurice and his legion famously refused to attack fellow believers, telling Caesar: 'Emperor, we are your soldiers but we are above all servants of God . . . You order us to put Christians to death. Search no further, here we are!'[8]

Systematically all 7,000 members of the Theban legion were executed by their own emperor for refusing to break their vow of allegiance to Christ the King. It is on the site of this atrocity that a later king, Sigismund, established the monastery in AD 515 as a place of 24–7 prayer in memory of the Theban legion and inspired by Alexander's Acoemetae.

Bangor Abbey (558–810)

It was around this time, as the Acoemetae continued to pray 24–7 in Turkey, alongside the *laus perennis* on the site of St Maurice's martyrdom in Switzerland, that a young missionary to Ireland received a vision of angels in a verdant Irish valley. And here, in St Patrick's Valley of Angels, a Christian community was established which would grow into one of the most influential houses of prayer not just in Ireland but right across Europe. For most of its life, Bangor Abbey almost certainly prayed 24–7, continuing until the Vikings ransacked the community in 810, killing 900 people in a single day.

Bangor's prayers powered a remarkable missions movement from Ireland right across Europe as far as Bulgaria and Ukraine in the heart of the Dark Ages. And like many other houses of prayer, Bangor Abbey became renowned as a seat of great learning and education.

Columbanus (559–615)

One of the many young men educated and sent out

from Bangor was the Celtic saint Columbanus, who took the gospel back to Gaul (modern-day France), establishing four great monasteries, all of which conducted the *laus perennis*. Hundreds of monks looked to Columbanus for leadership and his influence became so profound that one king begged him not to leave the country until he had converted the population there!

The Wesley brothers

After the Reformation, we see the 24–7 prayer model continuing to influence national and international affairs. No doubt inspired by the Moravians, John Wesley gathered friends to pray through the night on 1st January 1739. Famously he recorded in his Journal how 'about three in the morning as we were continuing instant in prayer the power of God came mightily upon us in so much that many cried out for exceeding joy and many fell to the ground'.[9]

The Wesley brothers were shot out like rockets from that prayer meeting and were soon joined by George Whitefield. As they preached, prayed and strategised, revival fires began to spread across the British Isles and across the Atlantic in New England alongside Jonathan Edwards. It was a revival in the truest sense of the word, resulting in profound social change, most notably the abolition of slavery, as well as massive numbers of people turning to Christ.

Modern times

When William Booth founded the Salvation Army in 1865, the movement was marked by its marriage of practical care for the poor and destitute with its passion for prayer. Booth, no doubt recalling Wesley's example,

> 'people were struck down, overwhelmed with a sense of the presence and power of God'

would hold all-night prayer meetings in which 'people were struck down, overwhelmed with a sense of the presence and power of God'. Over the following hundred years, as the Moravian prayer watch drew to a close, God began raising up other prayer movements to take its place. In the latter years of the nineteenth century there was a great stirring of intercession all over the world, from the Moody Bible Institute in America to Mukti School in India, via the Keswick Convention in England.

And in the opening years of the twentieth century, it was in answer to centuries of persevering prayer that we witnessed the most remarkable global outpouring of the Holy Spirit since Pentecost. Revival movements shook Wales, Scandinavia, India, Indonesia and many other parts of the world. Missionaries from Europe and America gathered in Edinburgh to strategise world evangelisation, and as they did so God was already planning his next great move. It had begun in a back street of Los Angeles with a 24–7 prayer room. Here, at 312 Azusa Street, men, women, even blacks and whites mingled freely, praying night and day for three years. By the summer of 1906 Pentecostalism had been born in this unlikely prayer room and the rest is quite literally history. Few generations have come closer to fulfilling the Great Commission, and it took two bloody world wars to hold them back.

Back to the future

Recent years have seen many other expressions of 24–7 prayer:

- The unprecedented global coalition of prayer for the '10–40 window'
- Pastor Cho's famous prayer mountain in Seoul, Korea
- Mike Bickle's International Houses of Prayer based in Kansas City
- Sister Kim Collins' Roman Catholic Burning Bush movement, with offices in Rome
- The Call, which fills stadiums around the world for days of non-stop prayer and fasting

These are just a few examples of a global phenomenon – a mass movement of prayer over recent years. (Of course, some of the most significant prayer gatherings shall undoubtedly remain unknown until we get to heaven.) And alongside all of this there's us – 24–7 prayer – just one fractal of a much bigger pattern that God is designing in our time.

Looking back at the impact of previous seasons of sustained prayer we have cause to be very excited right now as we witness such a global mobilisation of prayer. Viewing history with the eyes of faith we can see the ebb and flow of God's purposes in the world through his praying people:

- He heard Anna's life-long prayer vigil in the temple night and day, as well as that of the disciples in the Upper Room of Pentecost, who had met in obedience to his command (Acts 1:4), and so at a moment in time in answer to prayer he gave us the church.
- He heard the prayers of the Acoemetae, St Maurice, Bangor Abbey and Columbanus, altering the destiny of Europe as the Roman Empire decayed.
- He heard the prayers of the Moravians and stirred revival in England, Ulster and America.
- He heard the prayers of the late nineteenth and early twentieth centuries, pouring out his Spirit with global consequences.

And now, as we pray together, connected as never before by modern technology, we can be sure that God hears; that our prayers rise up to his throne like the incense from the golden bowl in the tabernacle and the temple; that as we persevere, in humble and united prayer, God will hear from heaven, send the rain and heal our land (2 Chronicles 7:14).

Joining the queue

Tracing so many examples of incessant prayer down so many years (only a few of which we have been able to mention here), we began to realise that 24–7 prayer has been God's idea from beginning to end. He has always mobilised movements, moments and entire communities like us to intercede without ceasing. Isn't it amazing to think that by giving ourselves to 24–7 prayer in this way, we are actually standing in a long and remarkable line of Christian community, raised up to intercede in every generation until Christ returns?

Watch and pray

> 'Could you . . . not keep
> watch with me for one
> hour? . . . Watch and pray
> so that you will not fall
> into temptation.'
> (Matthew 26:40-41)

It was his darkest moment, there in the Garden of Gethsemane, and Jesus needed his three best friends like never before. Instead, they slept. As we keep watch through the hours, the tides and the seasons of testing and turmoil, we draw near to Jesus in a very special way.

This model of watchfulness and presence was the very heartbeat of tabernacle and temple, represented by the flame that burned continually on the altar. The priests, with their faithful schedule of worship and sacrifice, maintained that flame of God's presence perpetually for generations. It was to them the very heart of the nation, a microcosm of the universe itself. Isaiah predicted a people who would one day give themselves no rest and give God no rest until he establishes Jerusalem and makes her 'the praise of the earth' (Isaiah 62:6–7). Jesus himself lived a life of perfect watchfulness, continually attentive to his Father. This often meant praying right through the night (Luke 6:12).

And beginning with the Upper Room in Jerusalem, God's people have been inspired ever since to maintain prayerful vigil, creating communities and environments of intentional intimacy with our Father in heaven. Here we can wait on God, walking and talking with him as we did once upon a time in the Garden of Eden. Here we can wrestle with darkness, as our Saviour did in the Garden of Gethsemane. Here we can worship, glimpsing the day when heaven will come to our communities as it has to our hearts. For ever.

Chapter 5: The big idea
- TURNING THE TIDE

'Is it true today
That when people pray
Clouded skies will break
Kings and queens will
shake?'
(Delirious? - 'History
Maker')

In the last chapter we explored the mass movement of prayer, called forth by God, of which 24–7 is just a part. God has particularly called us to focus our prayers on the emerging, postmodern, Western generation. Our dream is to play our part in turning the tide of youth culture back to Jesus. It's a big dream, which some would say is impossible. . . .

Turning the tide

According to legend, the ancient (Danish) King Canute

tried to turn back the tide. Positioning his royal throne on the seashore one day, he began to shout at the waves with all the authority he could muster as the tide swept relentlessly in towards him. It didn't work and soon he was very wet. God:1; Canute:0.

Right now the tide of Western culture is surely approaching its lowest ebb. Suicide rates are rocketing among young men. Eating disorders and other self-image problems affect women everywhere. Materialism and greed seem to determine everything. And the body of Christ is bleeding young people. But, of course, at the moment of lowest ebb, the tide turns with greatest force.

> 'I believe as a 59-year-old woman, sitting in this prayer room, that if these young people are the next generation, our land and our world is in safe hands.' (Liz)

The tides and seasons of our lives are not determined by powerful people like Canute, and not even by modern media icons worshipped by millions. Human destiny ultimately rests in the heart of God and the hands of his people. That is why we must pray. Again and again we have declared our intention to be 'history makers in this land'. Perhaps it's in response to this prayer that God is gathering this army of young intercessors.

History shows that this is an amazing time to be alive. When the early church spread from that prayer room in Jerusalem to the ends of the earth it was a sociological phenomenon as well as a spiritual one. The Roman Empire's network of nations, roads and ideas created a matrix for the incredible spread of the gospel. Of course, the printing press did the same for the revolutionary ideas of Martin Luther's Reformation.

In the same way, today's Internet/MTV generation represents a new empire of trade routes by which the gospel of Jesus could easily spread around the world. Right now it's an empty vacuum just filled with stuff like Coke and McDonald's. People are hungry for something more . . .

'Anything not born in prayer is born in pride.'

But strategy alone will not achieve this. As Joy Dawson says, 'Anything not born in prayer is born in pride.' Perhaps the greatest need of this hour is for Christianity to become contagious once again. And this Jesus epidemic begins in his presence, in the blood and not the head. It's time for us to lay down our differences, join hands around the world and pray as he taught us.

If Zinzendorf's 24–7 prayer meeting in an obscure village could impact the earth, perhaps that could happen where you live too! God has not changed. The Moravians prove to us that the tide really can turn right across nations and generations. The sea of popular opinion does not listen to kings on their thrones who shout at the waves. The tide turns when nobodies like us unlock the power of persistent, faithful and focused prayer.

In the next section, we get really practical about how you can do 24–7 where you live.

'Yes it's true,
and I believe it,
I'm living for you.
I'm gonna be
A history maker
in this land . . .'
(Delirious? - 'History
Maker')

SECTION 2:

HOW TO RUN A
24-7 PRAYER ROOM
(THE PRACTICAL BIT)

Introduction to the practical bit

This section of the book is designed to answer all your most practical questions and help you run the wildest prayer meeting ever! We're here to help you turn the dream of 24–7 prayer into a reality where you live. With this book and CD-ROM, as well as our online resources and telephone helpline, we're here to walk you through the planning stages of 24–7, into your prayer room and out the other side!

Join the club

We can guarantee that right now someone somewhere is praying 24–7, and your group can be a vital link in this international chain for just a few days or many months.

- 24–7 is for groups who know that God is calling them to pray . . . but are bad at it! It takes normal, disorganised people and teaches them to pray – by praying.

- 24–7 is for all ages, but is particularly focused on young people (the church family's missing generation). There's an awesome sense of being caught up in something God is doing in our time. He has started it. He will make it happen.

Keep it simple

Star Trek's Mr Spock would never have approved of 24–7 – it is entirely ridiculous at every level! So don't get too complex (or 'sensible') about it. All you really need to do is find a room with a kettle, mobilise the troops and start to pray.

After reading this book you may feel fully tooled up to just get on with doing 24–7 without any further help. If that's the case, great! But if you're still unsure, there are loads more great resources available:

- from any of our websites (listed at the back)
- through our UK telephone helpline (08710 97 11 99) dedicated to prayer room organisers like you
- from the CD-ROM accompanying this book

Registering your prayer room

In order to keep connected as a movement, we do invite groups to register the dates of their prayer room with us. Registering means that we can keep growing as a movement, tracking all the prayer rooms and building community by sharing our experiences, encouragements and prayer requests. It also helps individual prayer rooms feel part of the big global picture. What's more, when you register you receive loads of cool stuff:

- A FREE pack of useful resources in the post
- A DISCOUNT on our most popular prayer room resources
- International PROFILE for your group by being featured on our website

C'mon, let's stay together . . .

It only takes a minute to register your prayer room and you can do it in one of two simple ways:

- Online at www.24-7prayer.com/register
- By post, returning the card inside the CD wallet

If after reading this book you have any further questions, no matter how detailed, please don't hesitate to get in touch with a member of the team at your nearest 24–7 base (contact details are at the back of this book). If there is no 24–7 base in your nation, please contact the international base instead.

'Our 24-7 week exceeded all
expectations. Over 200
people used the prayer
room, and more than 20
churches got involved.
24-7 has been one of the
most productive (yes,
prayer is productive!)
weeks I have ever known.
People were saved. The
lukewarm were ignited.
Unity made huge steps
forward. Through 24-7, a
radical vision was impart-
ed way beyond anything
our puny little talks could
have accomplished. The
week has also multiplied
itself into three other
locations.' (Ian)

Step 1:
Planning your prayer room

'We left the prayer room at 4.35am, madly and passionately in love with Jesus.'
(Sarah)

It's important to build up to a season of prayer with careful preparation. There are a number of key questions to take into consideration at the planning stage:

- How long should we go for?
- When should we do 24–7?
- Why do we need a prayer room?
- Where should we locate our prayer room?
- What should our prayer room look like?
- What should we put in our prayer room?

How long should we go for?

Some groups start with a 24-hour vigil or a weekend of

prayer, but most can quite easily manage a week or more right from the start. In deciding how long to go for, take the following considerations into account.

The size of the group

As a rough guideline, you only need 30 people to commit to pray for an hour a day to fill a week with non-stop prayer (after all, 1.2 billion Muslims are currently praying five times a day!). This assumes that a few will pray in pairs, while the majority prefer the room to themselves.

The strength of the community

In our experience, the biggest factor in making 24–7 work for a sustained period is *not* the size of the group but the strength of the community. Some really big famous churches have struggled to do a single week of 24–7 – probably because their people aren't accustomed to attending anything other than Sunday services. Meanwhile a close-knit group of just 20 students in Belfast found it so easy to pray for a week they kept going for another one!

The maturity of the group

A Taiwanese believer told us that he was going to get his small cell group to do 24–7 for an entire month. Our UK base was worried that he was being over-ambitious until we learned that most members of this guy's cell group had been beaten severely by their parents for daring to get baptised. Some had even come to him needing hospital treatment. Our friend pointed out that having counted the cost of commitment in this way, a daily prayer hour was not going to be a big deal for them at all.

The international aspect of 24–7 often proves humbling for those of us in the West. We have discovered that if you're a Brazilian believer, the funniest part of this book will probably be the section encouraging people to consider fasting from chocolate for a week. These guys, many of whom have fasted from food for a whole month, tend to make fun of our low pain thresholds!

Sometimes, however, people do struggle to motivate a church to do 24–7 – not because the group is lukewarm but rather because the person with the vision for it is failing to communicate and plan effectively. There are tips on motivating and mobilising others in Section 3.

The pace of prayer

24–7 prayer is meant to be a challenge, so don't be too cautious in your planning. Believe it or not, some groups can't stop at the end of their planned time and keep praying for weeks or even months longer than they first expected!

If you're too cautious in your planning there will always be several people in the prayer room at any given moment, which isn't ideal because most people prefer to pray alone.

One pastor planning a week of prayer cleared much of his diary, expecting to have to cover a lot of empty slots. He never actually managed to get one at all, such was the demand!

We've also noticed that a certain momentum often builds up as prayer weeks progress. Groups that aim too low at the planning stage miss this exciting discovery of mounting momentum and even breakthrough.

However, if in doubt it's better to go for a week and end up doing two rather than announce plans that you are going to pray for a month and then quit after a fortnight! And if your week doesn't work out, don't panic. Just stop. You've probably still prayed more than ever before and we're not trying to break any records.

When should we do 24–7?

Choose the week carefully, taking the following factors into consideration:

- Local commitments. Are your key people going to be around?
- Does it clash with other commitments either in the church calendar or in the wider community (such as school holidays or exams)?
- Could your prayer room build up to an evangelistic focus or form part of a missions push?
- Think ahead. See the prayer season as part of the bigger picture of your church life. You might want to pray for one week fairly soon and then a longer period later in the year.
- Many churches are building regular seasons of 24–7 into their ongoing community life. At Revelation

Church in the UK we've experimented loosely with a cycle that passes from:

– a season of prayer
– into a season of mission
– into a season of fun (in which we keep meetings to a minimum, celebrating friendship and family together) before passing back
– into a season of spiritual intimacy in the 24–7 prayer room.

Why do we need a prayer room?

We think it is really important to locate your prayer in a fixed location for loads of reasons:

- The Holy Spirit can fill a place as well as a person (Acts 2:2).
- The sense of God's presence after many hours of prayer makes prayer easier and the time pass much more quickly. Many people have reported that in the prayer room one hour feels like ten minutes, where-as at home ten minutes of prayer often feels more like an hour!

> 'Wow! I didn't believe all that stuff about one hour being like ten minutes, but it's true . . . People don't want to leave!' (Dave)

- Our culture is looking for holy places – locations of sanctuary and spirituality which rarely equate in the postmodern imagination with a two-hour singing session in a purpose built venue on a fixed day of the week. Jenny Robertson writes: 'There is, in fact, a tremendous hunger now in the West to rediscover holy places. Places where tragic accidents happen are quickly turned into shrines, with flowers, candles, toys, photographs of the child struck down in a car accident, of the victim of a violent crime.'[10]

- Evangelistically the prayer room is excellent. Non-Christians have often sat in such places to pray, and some have said that they can feel God's presence. As we noted earlier, people who don't want to be preached at may still like to be prayed for.

> 'A prayer room helps a church look beyond itself, motivating it to unleash prayer power for the unsaved, the community, the nation, the church's missionaries, and the world.'[11]

- Creative and unusual environments can be highly conducive to prayer. The prayer room enables people to pray non-verbally, by posting artwork, poetry and graffiti on the wall. The environment can be designed artistically to stimulate and direct prayer.

- The room provides accountability – a place where people have to turn up – and this ensures a constant flow, as one prayer shift hands the baton on to the next. Visiting the room is like a mini-pilgrimage.
- A shared location provides a strong sense of being part of a community carrying each other's burdens, as well as celebrating breakthroughs together. You are more than an invisible link in a telephone prayer chain.

> 'I told a non-Christian friend about our prayer room. She said, "My head's messed up right now, and I think I need to do some praying." I didn't realise she meant "right now" literally, until she left the club, went to the prayer room and spent two-and-a-half hours alone with God!' (Claire)

Where should we locate our prayer room?

We love the fact that prayer rooms are found in so many surprising locations. It's great to be getting the prayer out into the heart of communities like Swiss skaters, British police officers and American naval cadets, to name just a few examples. But think through the practicalities when selecting a suitable venue:

- *Accessibility.* Choose somewhere central for those travelling in at night.
- *Size.* Ideally the room should be big enough to move around in (there are a lot of prayer 'pacers' out there!) and big enough to take groups without being so cavernous that there's little scope for atmosphere and intimacy. A medium-sized room divided into themed areas works well.
- *Security.* How safe is the building? Think especially about late at night. Try to have a telephone available for emergencies (but switch the ringer off!).
- *Facilities.* Obviously you need toilets.
- *Noise/Disturbance.* With people coming and going all the time and music being played at all hours (see below), try to find a venue that is 'neighbour-friendly'. If it has to be in a private house, can you use a detached one or a basement?

What should our prayer room look like?

There are no rules – only principles that help create an environment conducive to prayer. Our world is going crazy right now with interior design programmes on television and New Age feng shui experts making a living from moving things around in the houses of people with too much money. It's high time we used our imaginations to create spaces that glorify God and help people meet him.

If this isn't your forte, commission some arty types to design the room so that it has a real impact when people step inside. (For more ideas see Section 3.) You will need a small budget for art materials, drinks, etc. If you do mobilise a team of people to design the room, start off by sharing with them any ideas you have about themes you want the room to explore. For example if it is holiness, you might consider creating a large altar and having an area by the door where people can take off their shoes as a symbolic response to holy ground.

Walls

Unless you're in a windmill or a lighthouse (!), you will probably have four walls to your prayer room. You can use each wall to direct people's prayers in a new direction. For example you could have:

1. A 'welcome wall' near the door, providing people with a visual introduction to the prayer room, its themes and aims. On this wall you should also have all the practical stuff like the all-important 'sign-up' sheet (where people write their names to reserve one-hour shifts – see later). You should also post a clear sign saying who's 'on call' for that particular 24-hour period (see later).

2. A 'wailing wall', where people can post personal prayer requests – a bit like the way the Jews do to this day, wedging their heart-cries on scraps of paper between the great bricks of the old temple in Jerusalem. You could also encourage everyone to post network

maps on this wall (spider graphs) listing all their non-Christian friends, family and work/school/college colleagues. This wall often becomes one of the most moving parts of any prayer room, depicting visually the deepest prayers of the community, laid out before God.

3. A 'worship wall', full of verses, images, scents and colours; anything to provoke wonder and praise. Prayer is not just a matter of asking God for things. It's about waiting upon him, lost in 'wonder, love and praise'.

4. A 'world wall' with an outward focus, perhaps featuring a world map, newspaper clippings, the details of specific nations, missionaries known to you, community issues in your local schools and among the poor. Some groups have even liaised with their local police and social services for prayer requests.

The centre of the room

The space between those four walls should not be left bare! Think creatively about what to put in the room itself (see later for a list of suggestions). You could dream up different sections with distinct 'prayer stations' leading people in ten-minute steps on a one-hour journey around the room. Some groups drape tents inside their prayer rooms, creating lovely little spaces where people can hide away with a Bible by themselves. Others divide up the space with sheets.

Lighting

The lighting should be warm and subdued. If you use candles, please make very sure that they are safe – nowhere near anything flammable – and that there is a fire extinguisher to hand. Lava lamps are great.

What should we put in our prayer room?

Stock the prayer room with anything that will stimulate the five senses, helping people – especially children – to pray with all of their being. Too often we close our eyes to pray, shutting out God's extraordinary sensory world. Perhaps he wants to teach us to pray with our eyes open. Here are just a few suggestions of things you could put in your prayer room, but please don't be intimidated by this list. You don't have to do all of them!

> 'Perhaps he wants to teach us to pray with our eyes open.'

Sound

- CD player and a broad choice of CDs (don't forget to provide music for the kids too). 24–7 produces a range of prayer CDs in different styles.*
- Instruments. You may want to provide a bongo drum, rain stick or guitar for people to use.
- You or another leader could record a 30-second

audio (or video) introduction, welcoming people to the prayer room, explaining why you are praying in this way and helping people to focus.

Sight

- Books
  - A Bible (obvious, but easy to forget!).
  - A book of prayers.
  - A 'share' book (such as an empty exercise book) where people can put their thoughts, answered prayers, and stories (put this somewhere very obvious).
  - *Operation World*, a prayer guide to every nation on earth by Patrick Johnstone and Jason Mandryk.*
- Visuals
  - If you're feeling really adventurous you could make a one-hour video guide leading people through their prayer shift in real-time, with regular pointers and Bible verses interspersed by helpful music. This might particularly focus in on local issues and world news items.
  - Alternatively, provide helpful tapes such as the Transformations series.*
  - Slide projections are great – perhaps of stunning scenes from creation (no family holiday snaps!).
  - Is there someone who could make a video of your area or even loop an old bit of film to project on the wall?
  - A world map or a globe.

- Posters
  - If your church has received any significant prophetic words or Bible passages you could make them into a poster.
  - It's worth printing out some relevant parts of the 24–7 website, such as topical prayer pointers, meditations, and pages from Operation World (www.24-7prayer.com/ow).
- Literature
  - A local newspaper.
  - 24–7 postcards and Supporter's leaflets.*
  - Prayer letters from people or projects in the church.
  - Copies of 24–7News.* (These really help people understand the bigger picture they are part of and inspire many to pray. You can download them from the web or get full colour copies free – just pay postage.)
  - Post a selection of 60-minute prayer guides in the room. These should be focused around certain issues and take people on a spiritual journey, broken down into five-minute chunks (available with the 24–7 Start-up Pack* or make your own).

Touch

- Lots of paper (large sheets) and pens, paints, brushes, etc.
- Beanbags and comfy chairs.
- Some symbolic objects or pictures you can place in the room to direct people's prayers.

- Prayer slugs. We once built a massive 'prayer slug' from sheets of plastic and hoops. In the 'slug' people put prayers they had prayed and names of people they were praying for to show that they were given to God.
- A paper shredder for shredding sins written down on paper at the foot of a cross!
- A 'sin bin' (literally).
- A Labyrinth/Prayer Journey kit.*
- A giant pod. This is a large inflatable 6'/1.2m sphere which people can climb into and roll around like a giant hamster wheel! They're fun and cool in a prayer room (not cheap though!). Available from www.iwantoneofthose.com

Taste

- Drinks – especially tea and coffee.
- Salt, bread, cool water – the Bible is full of flavours laden with significance.

Scent

- Air freshener (prayer rooms do tend to get a bit musty after a few days).
- Incense sticks.
- Fresh coffee (see above).

Practical items

- Kettle, disposable cups, etc.
- Blu-tak, thumb tacks, dust sheets.
- Bin liners.

- The 'sign-up' sheet.* You need a large chart dividing each day into one-hour slots, where people can sign up to use the room (a template is included in our Start-up Pack*). Locate this at the back of every public meeting in the build up to the prayer room, with a persuasive person 'recruiting' (don't just expect this to fill up by itself)! At all other times the chart should be displayed in the prayer room so people know who is coming to relieve them and so others can come and sign up for slots during the week. (Some groups have developed an online sign-up rota, which can be particularly helpful in cities where people are commuting a long way to meetings, making it hard for them to 'pop in' during the week and book or cancel a slot.)
- A board giving the name and number of a person 'on call' in an emergency.

*Available from www.24-7prayer.com/shop

Checklist

☐   Decide on a date for your prayer room.
☐   Book a venue.
☐   Commission a décor team.
☐   Begin to inform local churches.
☐   Get useful resources.

Step 2:
Preparing a group to pray non-stop

'People are being discipled by the Holy Spirit. One girl who is a very new Christian visits the prayer room every day.' (Belfast, N. Ireland)

It's one thing to plan your prayer room, but quite another to mobilise the troops to make use of it night and day! Even if you caught this 24–7 vision quickly, most people won't. It takes weeks of careful communication to really inspire and mobilise most groups to get involved. 'Drip-feed' the vision of 24–7 over a period of time. Circulate 24–7 resources and perhaps arrange to play one of the short videos from the attached CD-ROM at a meeting while making an announcement.

In many ways, preparing people to pray is the most important job of all. God is not a massive slot machine into which we merely feed our prayers. There will be answers to prayer, but there will also be passionate prayers that seem to go unanswered. The point is that this is a space for people to hang out with their heavenly Father, a place of intimacy and transformation. In his presence we are changed – we become an answered prayer.

Communicate well with leaders

Whatever your official role in the church/group, it will be vital to communicate effectively with those who hold different areas of responsibility. Work hard at getting them on board and ideally actively involved. Sometimes senior pastors are nervous of 24–7 until they see it in action. They then invariably melt! Do try to keep the church calendar as free as possible for this season.

> 'Sometimes senior pastors are nervous of 24–7 until they see it in action.'

Teach on prayer

In the weeks leading up to 24–7 you will want to teach about prayer and get everyone excited about what God can do. Teach very practically. You could use the Lord's Prayer as a good model, and recommend books. On the website there are some recommended books and free materials you can download. If you have cell or home groups, focus them on prayer. Encourage people to share stories of answered prayer in order to build faith. Our Start-up Pack is specifically designed to inspire and ignite small groups for 24–7 and can be ordered from the website.

Many people think they won't be able to pray for a whole hour. Encourage them in the use of art materials and prayer pointer sheets. Explain that time will probably go quicker in that room. It is really important to excite the whole of the church and to get everyone involved, but in all of this make sure that you have particularly captured the hearts of your young people, as they are at the heart of 24–7.

Prayer pledges

It is a good idea, about two weeks before the launch of the prayer room, to invite people to pledge a certain number of hours per week, perhaps as an active response to a talk on prayer. Sometimes we actually ask people to write down their commitment on paper as a way of holding themselves to account. This certainly makes it easy to ensure that slots are filled. However, do remember that 24–7 is a grace thing from beginning to end; an opportunity rather than an obligation to pray. So no pressurising people or sending them on guilt trips, please! You could give people a symbol to remind them of their pledge throughout the week: a bracelet or a small sticker for their watch, for example. The 24–7 website sells US military-style dog tags with prayer slogans on them, and these are available in bulk for this very purpose.

Fasting

It's good to encourage a season of corporate fasting throughout the prayer time. It could be fasting from chocolate, make-up, alcohol, sex, TV or food (watch those with eating disorders). It is good to explain the power of fasting when combined with prayer.

Focus

Be clear about the objectives of the prayer week. You need to focus on local and personal needs, but beyond this the focus is on turning the tide in youth culture. The website provides all sorts of prayer resources you can print out around this theme.

Website

Wherever possible get members of the church to check out the 24-7 website and add it to their 'favourites' before the week starts. This often does more than anything else to excite and motivate them. If you have the technology, project the website onto the wall of your Sunday meeting when you share the vision.

'Thanks to the 24-7 website I can now say that I am a Christian.' (Claire)

Principles

Please keep rules to an absolute minimum in the prayer room. However, one or two principles are important:

- Variety. Let people pray how they want to. One night we had a guy praying silently to Celtic music, followed by a group dancing their prayers to disco tunes! Some like to shout and yell, pacing up and down. Some kneel quietly. Some paint. Some sing out Scripture or write their prayers down. Hour by hour the prayer style is as different as the people who are praying. It is all good stuff, and stops things getting boring for God! (OK, I jest.) It's a great strength of the 24–7 model that such diversity can be brought together in a single prayer meeting. Even Catholics and Presbyterians in Northern Ireland can participate together, one after the other, in the same prayer room.

> 'Hour by hour the prayer style is as different as the people who are praying.'

- Teenagers. What is your plan in terms of teenagers coming out at night? You could either put an age restriction on this or get older ones to come out with them. You might need to organise parental consent forms and strict guidelines. A good model is to get a whole cell group of teenagers to do a sleep-over in a room adjoining the prayer room with a responsible adult, where they can wake each other for prayer watches throughout the night.

- Children. By providing art materials and kids' praise tapes, all children can enjoy using the prayer room with a parent or guardian during the day.
- Pairs. We recommend that at night/after dark, people pray in pairs, unless they specifically want the room to themselves. In this case, they should indicate this clearly on the signing-up chart. (We get people to draw a red box around their name if they would like private use of the prayer room.) Make sure that any regular church prayer meeting is also conducted in the prayer room.

In all this remember to follow your church or group's policy on child safety and protection – and if you haven't got one, you need to get one! In the UK, for instance, there are very clear guidelines under the terms of the Children Act about the number of adults who should be present with anyone under the age of 18.

'On-call' team

This is one of the vital keys to a successful prayer season. You will need to recruit a few reliable people to be your 'on-call' team. These people will each then be responsible for backstopping a 24-hour period of prayer. Their job is as follows:

- To fill empty slots. The day before their duty they should check the signing-up sheet to see if there are any blank slots where no one has signed up to pray. They should then phone around people in order to fill up these slots. (N.B. they need to be gentle in this. We do not want people feeling pressured into praying!) It is useful to build up a bank of people who do not mind being called out to pray in an emergency.

- To be on call. On their allocated day, the person is on call for 24 hours. They must be contactable throughout that period. (Ideally they need to have a mobile phone or pager.) Their contact number for that day should be posted clearly in the prayer room. We have found that it works better to start the on-call period at 9a.m. rather than midnight, as this saves people having to turn on phones in the middle of the night. The person on duty visits the prayer room at 9a.m. to write their name and number up on an 'on-call' board and check that everything's OK. Throughout the next 24 hours everyone who uses the room will know that this person is the one to call if there are any problems. If someone does not turn up for a prayer slot (yes, it does happen!), then it is the job of the person who is on call to fill the slot themselves or find someone else to relieve the previous person. This stops people ever feeling 'trapped' in a prayer room if the next person doesn't show.

- To tidy up. The person on call is to ensure that on

their day the room is kept stocked with tea, coffee, paint, etc. and is tidy. This is a daily task.

'His whisper is much louder in here.' (Jen, age 13)

Checklist

☐ Arrange for some teaching on prayer in at least one big meeting and in small groups.

☐ Consider taking 'prayer pledges' as a response.

☐ Gather an 'on-call' team and have a planning meeting.

Step 3:
Launching your prayer room

'We started off our week
with our agendas, then
slowly God led us to the
cross and then to the lost
- to his agenda. We've been
working for years here
(without much success) to
engender a real concern
for the lost among our
churches and young people.
Suddenly there's tears,
prayers and compassion,
and it's being lived out
when we get home. Yes, God!'
(Andy)

Grand kick-off

Put some thought into the actual launch meeting of

your prayer room. Make it a real event and start with a bang! This is something historic you are doing here.

Remember to have the sign-up sheet on display at the launch meeting so that people can still sign up for remaining vacant slots as they arrive (and later as they leave).

You might also consider projecting the 24–7 website onto the wall to show people where else in the world prayer is happening at the same time as you are praying and who's about to pass the baton of prayer on to you. 24–7 can sometimes offer teams to come and help launch prayer weeks, but our resources are limited and with a dozen new rooms launching every single week-end, we can't attend them all. However, do feel free to ask.

The best context for launching into prayer is worship. Make sure everyone knows exactly what time the prayer room will kick in and discipline the worship leader to keep his or her eye on the clock. There are a number of ways you could mark the actual moment that launches your church into non-stop prayer. For instance:

- You could ceremoniously light a candle that will burn throughout the time (but if you do so, please ensure fire safety measures).
- You could establish a phone link with a group that will be finishing as you start, and get them to pray for you down the telephone.
- You could count down the final ten seconds NASA-style, all together, and send the first person/people

to start praying as you reach 'lift-off'!

● If your launch meeting is in a different venue from your prayer room (and depending on the leanings of your church!) you could even crowd-surf the first people out of the venue on the count of ten to begin praying.

The launch event is just a fantastic opportunity to create momentum that will last for days in the prayer room. We've often observed that when a prayer room is well launched it continues to impact the group for a long time afterwards. You'll also be surprised at how many people are still only just beginning to get their heads around the 24–7 idea by the time of the launch – no matter how diligently you've sought to raise awareness hitherto!

> 'Jesus is so near in the prayer room. Sometimes all of us weep for the lost. People just want to pray – we don't have to urge them. We haven't seen loads of answered prayers yet, but we have received vision, passion and a love for our nation and for this generation.'
> (Ocke - Germany)

Checklist

- ☐ Make a large sign-up sheet.
- ☐ Attempt to fill the first 24 hours and at least a quarter of the rest of the week with prayer pledges.
- ☐ Plan and publicise your launch meeting.

Step 4:
Maintaining the flow

'Prayer itself is an art
which only the Holy Spirit
can teach us. Pray for
prayer. Pray until you can
really pray.'
(C.H. Spurgeon)

What if we can't stop?

Good problem! Keep it going as long as there is life in it. You may need to consider putting out a news sheet to circulate stories, words and updates around the community. Work at keeping the momentum through motivational and effective communication and an ongoing public profile. Some people will not get involved until the very last minute and will then be sad when it stops. After three months, we still had church members visiting the prayer room for the first time!

'They all joined together constantly in prayer.'
(Acts 1:14)

Continue to encourage people to visit the website regularly, as it will help build faith and enable people to feel part of something that God is doing all around the world. If things go crazy and you just can't stop, organise a regular review meeting with the 'on-call' team to take the pulse and decide whether to extend for another block of time. If it's getting hard to fill slots, stop!

Please don't announce that you are going to keep going indefinitely unless you have been building up to this for a long time. Otherwise, this is a recipe for ultimate discouragement, no matter how much short-term excitement it generates when you first make the announcement. If God is leading you in this direction, he will confirm it as you discuss the implications sensibly. If things are going well, extend a week or a month at a time. Remember: it's better to quit while you're ahead, leaving people hungry for more and excited about the next time, than to exhaust and cajole people.

What if some people are praying too much?

You can laugh, but it does happen! There is an addictive quality to the presence of God (check out Obed-Edom in the Old Testament) and some people have to be told to go home! We would suggest that no one ever does more than a three-hour stint unless they particularly want to conduct a night vigil. Clearly, God doesn't want anyone's home life or work to suffer.

Here's a great story about an over-zealous prayer warrior more than a thousand years ago:

'A brother came to the monastery of Abba Silvanus and when he saw all the brethren at work he said to the elder, "Do not labour for the bread that perishes. Mary has chosen the better part." At this the elder called a disciple and said, "Zachary, give this brother a book and show him to an empty cell." The ninth hour, which was the hour for dinner, came and passed. The guest was intently watching his door to see if someone would come and get him for dinner, but no one called him. At length he rose and went to find the elder. "Abba," he said, "are the brethren fasting today?" "No, they have all eaten," replied the elder. "Why wasn't I invited?" "Because," answered the elder, "you are a spiritual person and have no need of bodily nourishment. But we, carnal as we are, are obliged to eat and this is why we work. You, however, have chosen the better part; you read all day long and have no desire for bodily nourishment." At these words the man made a prostration and said, "I beg your pardon, Abba." The elder pardoned him and concluded his lesson with the words, "That is how Mary herself stands in need of Martha. It was because of Martha that Mary could receive her praise."'[12]

Feedback

Please do take the time to post reports and stories on www.24-7talkback.com throughout the week. Anything that gets written in your 'Share' book in the room is worth uploading onto the website, along with poems and stuff. This encourages people all around the world who are standing with you as you pray. If you email us updates, we can also post them on the site's 'news' section. And don't forget to update church members at your Sunday meetings!

> 'Be joyful always; pray
> continually.'
> (1 Thessalonians 5:16-17)

Checklist

☐   Keep your finger on the pulse of the prayer room through regular contact with your on-call team.

Step 5:
Ending your season of prayer

'Our church has been
changed for ever . . .
Dozens are coming back to
Jesus, or are being saved
and filled with the Holy
Spirit. We are believing
for an awakening that will
usher in the greatest
harvest the world has ever
seen. 24-7 prayer has
enabled us to be a part of
it.' (Ann Burns -
Tennessee, USA)

Finish with a bang!

It is really important to end your season of prayer decisively and joyfully with some kind of celebration.

- One group took all the artwork and graffiti from the walls of their prayer room and created a 'prayer bonfire' with all the paper. As they set light to it they offered all these heart-cries up to God in one great final blaze.
- A large and fairly conventional church in Tulsa, Oklahoma, created an extraordinary finale to their prayer time, surrounding the congregation with drummers whose rhythmic beats created a sonic backdrop while prayers from the room were read out. Some of these were painfully honest (almost too honest for such a large context) and others were nothing short of miraculous. The congregation that day found themselves caught up in an expression of corporate pain and praise unlike anything they had ever known before, which continued for more than an hour.
- In Mexico they just opened the doors of the room and threw a feast of fajitas and tortillas for all their friends.

We suggest you resist the (strong) temptation to keep the prayer room open indefinitely, available for occasional usage in between seasons of prayer – that is, unless it is an ongoing chapel. When Peter witnessed the transfiguration he instinctively wanted to build shrines, but this clearly was not Jesus' desire. As people encounter Christ in remarkable ways in the prayer room there may be similar inclinations, but we too want to avoid such a 'shrine' mentality.

Debrief

As well as finishing with some kind of celebration it's helpful to gather people for a simple debrief as you end your time of prayer. The debrief is a context for getting feedback, dealing with any disappointments, sharing the exciting stories and sounding everyone out about the possibility of doing 24–7 again some time.

Please let us have the following from your prayer room:

- *Encouraging stories*. Send in all clear answers to prayer. If they relate to miraculous healing, please ensure that these stories are checked out.
- *Art and poetry*. It would be great if every prayer room could try to contribute a couple of poems and pictures for the 24–7 gallery. Sadly we cannot return artwork, but you can send photos or email images directly to your local base or our international office as a JPEG or GIF file (all contact details at the back of this book).

> 'I cancelled work and even slept in the prayer room . . . It was just too wonderful to leave. This week has ended but our prayer room has just begun.' (Andy - Canada)

Money

There is no charge for doing 24–7 prayer and as you may already have noticed, we offer many of our resources at cost price or even free. This isn't easy. We're registered as a charity in a number of countries, including the UK, and rely on people's generosity month to month to keep the show on the road. If your group is blessed by 24–7 and would like to take up an offering to support us, we would really appreciate that. Such a donation would help to cover our costs in supporting you, and can also subsidise prayer rooms in poorer situations and countries closed to the gospel, where it is illegal to proselytise but impossible to prevent people praying. (Please make cheques payable to 24–7prayer.com or donate online.)

Support the team

You might also consider becoming a regular 24–7 Supporter. By making a modest monthly donation, you get password access to a dedicated area of the 24–7 website, where we share our most confidential prayer requests and news items. We also send all our Supporters a complimentary copy of 24–7news every couple of months to keep them in the loop as best we can. Our Supporters really are the very heart of 24–7, without whom we couldn't function. (See www.24-7prayer.com/support for more details.)

Local organiser's checklist

Don't panic! This list will help you run a successful 24–7 prayer room and summarises everything you've just read.

Now

- Publicise
    - ☐ Communicate with your church/group leadership.
    - ☐ Get as many people as possible logging on to www.24-7prayer.com.
    - ☐ Start to publicise 24–7 to your people and profile it at meetings.
- Plan
    - ☐ Locate a suitable prayer room.
    - ☐ Plan your launch meeting (the Sunday you start).
    - ☐ Recruit your 'on-call' team.

Next

- Recruit
    - ☐ Consider allocating 'sleep-over' nights to cell groups. Make sure that any regular church prayer meetings are booked into the room.
    - ☐ Get people signing up for hour slots at meetings.
    - ☐ Consider 'prayer-pledging'.
    - ☐ Get a team to decorate the room creatively.
    - ☐ Meet with your 'on-call' team.
- Prepare
    - ☐ Mobilise: brief cell-group leaders, teach on

prayer, get people excited!
- ☐ Consider using the 24–7 Start-up Pack.
- ☐ Order any extra supplies.

Launch meeting

- Communicate
  - ☐ Get as many prayer slots as possible filled (certainly the first 36 hours).
  - ☐ Explain how the week will work and any rules, etc.
  - ☐ Encourage *everyone* to use the website and update it during the week (show them where 'Wailing Wall', Operation World and 'Now Praying' are).
- Inspire
  - ☐ If possible, project www.24-7prayer.com onto a large screen.
  - ☐ You could play one of the songs from a 24–7 CD.
  - ☐ Count down and launch with a bang.

During

- Care
  - ☐ Lead by example!
  - ☐ Pastorally oversee. Deal with issues that arise.
- Communicate
  - ☐ Maintain daily contact with those on call.
  - ☐ Email reports to 24–7 on how it's going.
  - ☐ Post prayers on 'Wailing Wall' and stories/poetry/prophecy, etc. on 'Talkback'.
  - ☐ Take photos, especially of artwork.

After

- ☐ Consider taking up an offering for or making a donation to 24–7.
- ☐ Gather participants for a debrief.
- ☐ Feed back to 24–7.
- ☐ Send in artwork, photos, etc.
- ☐ Plan your next 24–7 season!

If you have any problems, we're always at the end of a phone. The 24–7 prayer room UK helpline is: 08710 97 11 99.

SECTION 3:

FIVE KEYS TO 24-7 (S.M.I.L.E.)
(THE TRAINING BIT)

Key 1:
Simplicity

Simply starting out in prayer

'Lord, teach us to pray.'
(Luke 11:1)

It's not easy, is it? Jesus' first disciples needed help with their prayer lives and so do we. Some people would rather climb Everest than pray for an hour. For others, the challenge is just to pray out loud.

A survey by the Teal Trust in 1998 discovered the worrying facts that 72 per cent of all Christians seldom attend a prayer meeting and 75 per cent of all Christian couples never pray together.

So don't just assume that all your people will step into the prayer room and know what to do. The room makes prayer easier, but not automatic! Even Jesus' disciples needed to be taught how to pray and what to say.

Prayer workshops

You could offer a prayer workshop in the room (or in an existing context) for people who want some tips on chatting to God. Our Start-up Pack has excellent cell materials designed to equip beginners in prayer. A workshop could go something like this:

● Seat the group in a circle. Create a relaxed atmosphere, bearing in mind lighting, music, room temperature and time, to welcome and relax people.
● Give a short initial piece of teaching on the power and the pleasure of prayer. Use personal examples of answered prayer and also be honest about your own struggles.
● Invite people to talk honestly in pairs about what they find difficult about prayer.
● Next, instead of going straight into a time of open prayer, help people gain confidence in praying out loud by giving everyone time to think up a prayer in advance (possibly writing it down). Gently make it clear that everyone will be expected to pray a short three-sentence prayer out loud – unless they opt out of the exercise before it starts.

'I feel inadequate to be here. I'm a pathetic prayer but you're pleased that I'm here. If you're pleased, then that's great, coz

> that's all that matters
> right now to a
> guy who longs to be doin'
> your will . . .'
> (Letter 2 God found in a
> prayer room)

How do I pray?

1. Accountability
An international survey discovered the top three barriers to prayer to be:

- wandering thoughts (80 per cent)
- noise and distraction (66 per cent)
- finding the time (54 per cent)

Well, don't panic – 24–7 can help with all three! The prayer room is a place away from noise and distractions, designed to help wandering minds to concentrate. And when you sign up for an hour's prayer slot, you know you're going to have to turn up if only because some-one will be waiting in the prayer room, unable to go home until you arrive! Being accountable for our private prayer lives in this way is good.

Many people also find it helpful to form a prayer partnership during 24–7. Grab a Christian friend – or even your boy/girlfriend (no kissing!) – for an hour with God.

2. Boldness

Dare to be yourself in prayer! Nothing's more scary than the idea of sitting in a circle for an hour in the 'shampoo position' (elbows on knees and hands in hair) while others pray long prayers, leaving even longer embarrassing silences in between.

Encourage people to be real with God in prayer. He can take it! Be honest. Talk about the things on your heart: not the religious things you think you ought to say, but the things you're really feeling.

Dare to be alone with God for an hour. It's actually much easier to concentrate and relax when no one else is listening.

3. Creativity

A man once stepped into a 24–7 prayer room with a big black Bible under his arm. As usual, artwork littered the walls, CDs and coffee cups were scattered on the floor

> 'Prayer is about using all our senses rather than shutting them down.'

and music was blaring from the stereo while people prayed in various ways. 'This atmosphere is *not* conducive to prayer,' he growled and stormed out. We understand that he was wanting a quiet, tidy and serene environment in which to pray, but we do believe that prayer is about using all our senses rather than shutting them down.

Encourage people to try lots of ways of praying. Try writing a song or a letter, painting a picture or reading a psalm. Experiment with different positions (standing, lying down, kneeling), different music (we generally don't think it has to be Christian, as long as it inspires you to pray), different books, like the Bible or Celtic prayers, and different ways of speaking: through noise, artwork, poetry. (For more on creativity, see Key 5.)

What do I say?

At Sunday school they used to teach the 'teaspoon' (tsp) approach to prayer, and it works for grown-ups too!

- **T**hank you. Start by giving thanks. Philippians 4:6 says, '. . . but in everything, by prayer and petition, with thanksgiving, present your requests to God.'
- **S**orry. Ask God to reveal to you specific sin in your life and then ask him to forgive you. This can open up the communication lines between you and God. It clears away the junk.
- **P**lease. Ask! Trust that he will hear you and answer. Be specific in your prayers.

Simplicity and spiritual warfare: ghostbusters

'Prayer is essential in this ongoing warfare. Pray hard and long. Pray for your brothers and sisters. Keep your eyes open.'
(Ephesians 5:16, THE MESSAGE)

There are all sorts of different types of prayer, ranging from quiet thanksgiving to noisy intercession. In 24–7 prayer you are taking a mixed group of people onto the front-line of spiritual warfare. It is important, therefore, that leaders take a careful, pastoral and balanced lead in all of this. On the one hand we must recognise that this really is a battle against principalities and powers (Ephesians 6:12). On the other hand we should create an atmosphere of safety and confidence in the prayer room, since we are 'more than conquerors through him who loved us' (Romans 8:37).

In case you are nervous about handling this side of things, here are a few dos and don'ts:

Do . . .

- encourage people to pray in pairs, unless they specifically want privacy, especially at night;
- give some basic teaching about our authority in Christ;
- provide simple prayer guidelines to lead people through the hour in a constructive way;
- trust God to protect and cover those who are immature and vulnerable.

Don't . . .

- allow sensational/spooky stories about the prayer room to circulate, generating fear (this does happen sometimes);
- allow the focus to become Satan. An atmosphere of worship will keep things on track;

- take on major spiritual powers over the nation/ area/generation unless it is in a mature context;
- allow weirdos to take over the room or generate an over-spiritual atmosphere!

> 'I am sending you out like sheep among wolves. Therefore be as shrewd as snakes and as innocent as doves.' (Matthew 10:16)

Key 2:
Mission

'For years I've been trying
to get my young people to
have a heart for the lost
and a desire to pray. Last
night I found eight of them
on their faces in the
prayer room at 2a.m.
weeping for their non-
Christian friends. What's
happening?' (Youth pastor -
Spain)

Mission: catching and carrying the virus

Prayer and outreach are inseparable.

- When the Holy Spirit fell at Pentecost, it was upon a
  prayer meeting and 3,000 got saved.
- The Moravian 100-year prayer meeting, tucked away

in a remote village in Germany, sent out 3,000 missionaries to the ends of the earth.

- Writing about the Hebridean (Scottish) Awakening of 1949–53, where entire communities came to Christ, Arthur Wallis observed: 'Let it be burned upon our hearts by the Spirit of God, that this mighty movement was not only born out of prayer, but that it brought forth prayer and was maintained by prayer.'

'The evangelization of the world depends first upon a revival of prayer.' (Robert Speers)

For this reason, it is a good idea:

- to focus your season of prayer on outreach, such as a forthcoming Alpha course or a university mission;
- to make sure that the room's design is outward-looking, with maps, newspaper clippings, photographs of missionaries, news of local schools and colleges and friendship networks, etc.;
- to encourage people to ask their non-Christian friends for prayer requests. Many of those who are closed to the gospel are open towards and appreciative of the offer of prayer. It only takes one miracle . . .;
- to consider knocking on neighbours' doors to gather prayer requests or arranging an anonymous 'prayer box' at school;

- to think about bringing a group to join a 24–7 prayer mission team in the high places of youth culture, praying non-stop, and seeking to love and to live like Jesus in some of the toughest spiritual environments on earth (check out the www.24-7 mission.com for details);
- to consider practical expressions of God's love and justice, like feeding the hungry or campaigning for debt relief.

'Lots of non-Christians have been visiting our prayer room. The first time they turned up they were a bit surprised to see their names on the wall where we were already praying for them! But instead of being freaked out, they decided to join in, and have been back a few times to pray for themselves.' (Roger Bretherton - Lincoln, UK)

Key 3:
Intimacy

Intimacy and priorities: one thing needed

Jesus watches Martha's hectic efforts to host him adequately with great concern. 'Martha, Martha,' the voice is kind but firm, 'you are worried and upset about many things, but only one thing is needed . . .' And with that he indicates Mary, who is apparently doing nothing at his feet.

As we have seen, 24–7 prayer is not just a good idea. It is a God idea. It's about waiting at Jesus' feet, realising that spiritual achievement has little to do with physical effort and everything to do with personal intimacy. In fact it's not really about doing anything at all; it's about being something – God's kids, his friends, his fiancée.

Identity crisis

> 'A prayer room is to the
> church what a heart is to
> the body.'[13]

The call to pray strikes at the very core of our identity as those made in the image of God; sentient beings created miraculously to walk and talk with our Maker in the Garden of Eden. Adam and Eve had work to do – making babies and naming animals – but it was not particularly taxing and it flowed out of friendship rather than function. But then we sinned, we filed for divorce, and suddenly work got harder, function overthrew friendship, relationships became fraught and childbearing now hurt like hell.

Life itself became a battle as creation spun into a cycle of decay. According to Romans 8, all creation still groans under the oppressive regime of sin, longing for those who will stand up and be counted as God's sons, agents of liberation and life amid so much death. That is how important intimacy with God is.

When Eve ate the forbidden fruit she began to avoid God, ashamed to be alone with him. In our sin we do the same: we hide from his presence, we run from prayer, we begin to build our identity around doing and achieving rather than talking and being with God.

Missing you already

When someone asks *who* we are, we all too easily tell them what we *do*. And yet in all our busyness, we often lose our identity and become lonely for God. When Mary chose to sit at Jesus' feet while her sister busied herself in the kitchen, she revealed something important about her priorities and her sense of identity. She had stumbled unwittingly back into Eden, where Adam and

Eve once walked and talked with God in the evening light. God remembers those days, and perhaps even he – the Alpha and Omega, the great I Am of everything – misses those times in the garden with his friends. Perhaps he is lonely for us as we are for him.

> 'quite honestly, if prayer is treated like another project in the diary we might as well not bother.'

Most church wall-planners are crowded enough already, without another assignment to add to the itinerary. And quite honestly, if prayer is treated like another project in the diary we might as well not bother. That's not what 24–7 is all about. A prayer room is a place where the wall-planners, the diaries and the rules of life become as irrelevant to us as they are to children. They are dispersed by eternity.

Enjoy

The Westminster Shorter Catechism encapsulates this issue of identity beautifully. Asking the ultimate question about the purpose of human life, it concludes: 'Man's chief end is to glorify God and to enjoy him for ever.' It took a committee five years to come up with that statement. Meeting from 1642 to 1647 to analyse the vast teachings of Scripture and the libraries of Judaeo-Christian theology, the Westminster Assembly eventually distilled it all into just 107 doctrinal statements. And the very first one asserts unequivocally that the purpose of life is intimacy, adoration and enjoyment of God.

> 'If we can't recognise the value of simply being alone with God, as the beloved, without doing anything, we gouge out the heart of Christianity.'
> (Brennan Manning, Author)

Intercessors anonymous

God is undoubtedly at this time looking for those who will make prayer their heartbeat rather than a thing they sometimes do as part of the Christian toolkit. It's about friendship rather than function; identity rather than duty. The book of Hebrews says that Jesus 'lives to intercede' and calls us to do the same: to participate actively and compassionately in his broken world. As we do so, we will often watch bewildered as the power of life is unleashed in our weakness. God is searching for those who will combine such intimacy with involvement, refusing to compromise either way, living to intercede in prayer and also in practice.

So many groups have already discovered that a regular season of 24–7 prayer is an absolute key to this identity – a metronome calling the community back to the feet of Jesus again and again in the busyness of life. Churches, universities, Bible colleges, mission teams – even businesses and schools – are building times of persistent prayer into their rhythm of life together. Time in

the garden with God. Time away from the kitchen to sit
at the feet of Jesus.

> 'We need to find God
> and he cannot be found in
> noise and restlessness.
> God is the God of silence.
> The more we receive in
> silent prayer
> the more we can give in
> our active life.'
> (Mother Teresa)

Intimacy and unanswered prayer:
Kevin's slot machine

OK, here's the scene . . . Kevin Keen (age 16) has decided
to get stuck into this 24–7 prayer thing. He's nervous
because he has never prayed for an entire hour in all his
life (except, maybe, one time outside the Head
Teacher's office). But he has been persuaded by his cell-
group leader that the time goes quicker in a prayer
room; that there will be music and art stuff and that
chatting to God is generally rather a funky thing to do.

Miracle 1
Major achievement. It's Saturday and Kevin manages to
drag himself out of bed at the crack of noon and down
to the prayer room before lunch.

Miracle 2
Kevin actually quite enjoys himself as he graffitis the phrase 'Satan Sux' in one-metre letters across the wall. He also designs a 'network chart' of all his non-Christian friends and relatives. Wanting his list to be the longest, he adds the names of his sister's pets and the members of Linkin Park.

Miracle 3
Kevin actually feels quite emotional when he writes up the name of his best mate Gavin. He would love it if Gav became a Christian. Hard to imagine though.

Miracle 4
On his way out of the room Kevin is surprised to find himself signing up for a slot praying at 3 o'clock Sunday morning. Later that day, the 'on-call' person notices Kevin's commitment and wonders whether his mum will be OK with him coming out in the middle of the night. A quick call reveals that Kevin's mum is delighted with her son's surprising commitment, provided he puts lights on his bike. Encouraged by Kevin's newfound devotion, she then offers to lend him her Keith Green LPs. Kevin looks confused and declines. Having phoned Kevin's mum, the diligent 'on-call' lady also notices that someone has written 'Stan Sux' on a five-metre length of paper. Stan being her husband's name, she pulls it down, wondering who would be so unkind and what Stanley could possibly have done to offend anyone so much.

Miracle 5
Kevin turns up at 2.59 a.m. (with bike lights).

Miracle 6
He loves it. He really, honestly, genuinely has a blast. He reads a bit of the Bible, writes a poem and sticks it on the wall. He jumps around to the Delirious? track 'Did You Feel the Mezzanine Floor Wobble?' and prays some more for Gavin. At 3.37 a.m. he gets a surge of faith and finds himself thanking God that 'Gavin is just like really going to get totally saved by Wednesday lunchtime, Lord'. The name of 'Gavin' resounds round that prayer room again and again. He can't find his graffiti anywhere.

Monday at school, Kevin tells Gavin all about the prayer room. Gavin actually seems quite interested and asks some questions.

On Tuesday Kevin informs Gavin that he has been actually, like – err – praying for him. Gavin goes quiet and looks at his shoes. Seems like a good sign. Kevin can hardly wait for Wednesday lunchtime when Gav is due to get saved. He spends most of the evening in the prayer room looking forward to Gavin's imminent conversion. Just before going home Kevin gets a picture in his head of a giant tuna fish singing a Matt Redman worship song.

Wednesday lunchtime Gavin is eating . . . tuna sandwiches. Excitedly Kevin points out to his friend that tuna is a fish and that the fish is the symbol of Christianity. He goes on to explain all about God and church, and especially the amazing vision of the giant singing tuna.

Discovering that he is expected to become a Christian before the end of his packed lunch, Gavin chucks his sandwiches on the floor, shouts something very rude at Kevin and storms off.

Kevin is gutted. He is angry at God. He has never prayed so hard about anything, ever. And he has never spoken up for God like this before. He decides to miss his cell-group meeting that night. Then he remembers that last week a total babe turned up for the first time and he changes his mind. He decides he will go, but will do so with attitude (in a cool, rock star sort of way).

Tracey (his cell leader) is one of those super-discerning types who know exactly what you're feeling even when you don't. As a result she misses the rock star thing completely and asks Kevin what's up. The whole sad, angry story comes out. Tracey listens, nodding her head sympathetically and saying 'mmm' a lot. When Kevin finishes spilling his guts she tells him that prayer doesn't work like a coin in the drinks machine. 'Gavin's a free agent,' she points out, 'and it's up to him whether he wants to be a Christian or not. Prayer helps change things, but it doesn't always make everything easy or automatic.'

' "Prayer helps change things, but it doesn't always make everything easy or automatic." '

Miracle 7
That night Kevin writes something unusually profound

in his Bible: 'Prayer is about talking to your Dad, not calling your dog.' He decides to share this at cell next week. But only if that new girl is there.

On Thursday, on his way home from school, Kevin reluctantly goes to the prayer room. Gavin hasn't spoken to him all day. Disguising his handwriting, he scribbles the most honest, angry prayer he has ever dared to write, and sticks it up on the wall.

Feeling better he prays once again for Gavin. 'Please, God, just get him to like me again.' And then Kevin Keen, aged 16, whispers something to God so quietly that no one anywhere in the world could possibly hear: 'OK, God. I want to be your friend even if Gavin doesn't, and even if he never, ever becomes a Christian, I guess I'll still follow you.'

Instantly, Kevin's tiny, whispered prayer echoes round the vast courts of heaven. His heavenly Father smiles, and whispers, 'Thank you, Kevin. And by the way, you're absolutely right about one thing: Satan does indeed suck.'

**Intimacy and the father heart of God:
wanna cuddle? (by Pete Greig)**

> 'For this reason I kneel
> before the Father . . .'
> (Ephesians 3:14)

I got a phone call from my two-year-old son a few days ago. I was miles from home, preparing to speak at a meeting. It was raining. I was tired. But when I heard that little voice on the line things seemed better. After chatting as usual about animal noises, 'wee-wees' in the potty and the Telly Tubbies, Hudson suddenly said something totally unexpected. He'd been feeling ill all day, but nothing could prepare me for the impact of his next sentence. He paused, then simply said, 'Daddy, I want a cuddle.'

Those childish words knocked the breath out of me. My eyes suddenly stung with tears. I would have done anything right then just to reach down the telephone line and gather that little boy in my arms. After all, he couldn't understand how far away I was – how impossible his request. For the first time in his little life his daddy couldn't show him love when he needed it.

As I joined the crowd at worship that night my heart was far away with a two-year-old boy. I watched people stretching out their arms to their heavenly Father as they sang, and I remembered Hudson's request for a cuddle from his daddy. How God must long just to reach down and gather us into his arms when we worship. And how I long for the day when I'll see my Father face to face.

It's an incredible buzz surfing this 24–7 wave. Again and again God has done 'immeasurably more' than all we could ask or imagine. Tens of thousands of young people are praying like never before. And it all started by accident. But the most amazing thing of all is not the many nations, the many miracles, the CD, the TV programmes or even the mission teams. The most amazing thing about 24–7 is that God wants to spend time with us so much that when we rise in the night, or lift our hands in the day, our Father in heaven responds again and again with such love, and gathers us into his arms.

> 'Night and day, in prayer rooms in many nations, the deepest heart-cry of the generation is the same: "Abba, Father."'

All the prayers come back to one simple longing: a kid asking his dad for a cuddle. Night and day, in prayer rooms in many nations, the deepest heart-cry of the generation is the same: 'Abba, Father.'

When we started praying non-stop in Chichester, UK, on 5th September 1999 God showed up. By the time we'd prayed for six weeks we felt sure that revival must be just around the corner. After all, we had never prayed so hard in all our lives. And then God brought us a man called John Dawson, who laid an important foundation stone into the prayer movement that was being born. He simply pointed out that everyone prays. Even non-Christians pray. The difference when Christians pray, however, is that they are climbing into the arms of their heavenly Father. That's why Jesus told us to begin our conversations with God, 'Our Father . . .'

It's true that we've seen incredible answers to prayer since all this began. In some places they are even experiencing genuine breakthrough as a result of 24–7. But the most important thing about every single prayer room, from Alaska to Australia, is that it is a place where people can be alone with their Dad. A place where you and I can study his features, find comfort in his love, learn to recognise his quiet voice, seek his advice and pour out our childish hearts to him. In the prayer room we pick up God's mannerisms, we grow in his likeness. We become the answer to our own prayers.

And of course that's the greatest miracle of all. 'Daddy, I want a cuddle!'

> 'In the prayer room God showed me the reality of his love. He showed me that he's my Daddy, which is an area that has been a struggle for me.' (Bryan, 16 - California, USA)

Key 4:
Leadership

Qualities of an effective prayer leader

24–7 works brilliantly when it has anointed leadership leading by example. It generally struggles when it doesn't have that. The ideal 24–7 organiser is good at motivating and mobilising people – especially young people – to do irrational things.

Jesus could say 'Come, follow me' in such a way that people actually wanted to do it! If you know that you're not gifted in this way, we suggest you team up with someone who is. They can do the public communication, while you build 24–7 on the ground. Secondly (and less importantly), a 24–7 leader needs to be able to organise the practical aspects of the room.

Your role is to lead by example. People will look on the 'sign-up' chart to see if you've been doing your time! Why not make the most of the opportunity and book out a night just to 'keep watch' alone with God? These are always amazing times to pray, read, meditate and reflect.

'Jesus considered prayer
more important than food.'
(Billy Graham - Mark 1:35)

Seasons of prayer

Of course, prayer should undergird everything we do, but life is crowded with so many legitimate demands upon our time. If 24–7 works for you, we would suggest that you build it into your ongoing church life in limited seasons to make space for other stuff. There's a time to pray, but also a time to act out those prayers. In nature, in Scripture, in the example of our forefathers, there is a seasonal rhythm to life. You might consider building your calendar around the cycle we mentioned earlier:

- A season of prayer (intimacy, intercession, reflection, worship, creative expression, self-discipline, fasting, etc.).
- A season of mission. This gives a focus to the time of prayer and a fruitful outworking of it evangelistically.
- A season of fun. A time with fewer meetings, where we have the space to enjoy being alive, to model the kingdom of heaven, to be with friends and family, and to renew our strength.

Key 5:
Expression and creativity

Creativity in prayer

One of the things that often takes people by surprise when they create space for 24–7 prayer is that there is an instant explosion of creativity. Instinctively, it seems, many people choose non-verbal ways of communicating with God the moment they have the opportunity. Suddenly prayers are painted, drummed, enacted, rhymed, choreographed and even sculpted.

It all seems a long way from the traditional prayer meeting in which hardy intercessors would (depending upon denomination) either sit around in a silent circle, listening politely to the occasional soliloquy in search of a whispered 'amen', or rant and stamp around with crescendos of tongues, yelling in somebody else's accent and apparently quite terrified of any silence or stillness whatsoever.

When one church launched a 24–7 prayer room, someone brought in a pile of rocks to symbolise something or other. One morning a sign appeared saying 'danger', provoking every person who came to the room for several days to go on their own little path of interpretation. Prophetic symbols abounded.

It is really important to encourage such creativity. We've spent 40 years re-energising the musical aspect of our worship with new songs, new instruments and sophisticated technical equipment in even the tiniest churches, and meanwhile prayer has been left behind, in need of a cultural and creative revolution.

The creativity of God is evident all around us, as is the inadequacy of speech amid the mysteries of life. How then can we reduce something as profound as prayer to mere words? Loving God demands the whole of our being: emotion, imagination and personality.

The very first person in the Bible to be described as being 'filled with the Spirit' was not one of the great prophets or patriarchs. It was a man named Bezalel, whose job was to decorate the prayer room, to adorn the tabernacle with symbols and colour (Exodus 31:2–5). Just as Bezalel's job was to decorate the holy place of worship, so today God wants prayer rooms to be places of creativity, and will anoint people with gifts to decorate creatively.

'Bezalel exhibits in miniature the divine creative role of Genesis 1 in the building of the tabernacle. The precious

> metals with which they
> work take up the very
> products of God's beautiful
> creation and give new
> shape to that beauty
> within creation.[14]

God has put in all of us the ability to be creative, inventive, imaginative. Prayer rooms are a fantastic way to create atmospheres and environments that help release people's imaginations and dreams.

A circle of plastic chairs is hardly conducive to prayer, so provide materials and plenty of wall space. Some groups even allow graffiti all over the walls, promising to whitewash them again at the end of the 24–7 prayer time. Practically, you may need to protect the floor. It's well worth buying a big roll of lining paper and a bulk load of sticky tape.

Art and soul

Occasionally inappropriate pictures or statements may appear on the wall, and if this happens just quietly remove them. You may become concerned that the art stuff is becoming a distraction from prayer for some people, rather than an expression of it. However, it is important not to be judgemental. After all, conventional expressions of prayer can distract us too. When praying aloud it's easy to become fascinated by the sound of our own voices 'praying to the gallery'. But no one would suggest that we desist from spoken prayer. Or perhaps people notice us communing serenely with God, eyes closed and head bowed, when in fact we have been hijacked by that worthy silence so that our mind is now lost on level three of Sonic the Hedgehog.

If people do paint to such an extent that they are no longer using their prayer times to converse with God in words, then they are probably being more lazy than creative! We don't want prayer rooms to become glorified art classes any more than we want them to be places for people to deliver 60-minute speeches to the ceiling. A gentle notice reminding visitors to engage with God verbally and consciously, as well as through art, normally resolves the imbalance very quickly.

In his letter to the Corinthians, Paul describes a similar tension between praying with the mind/with words/with rational thought on the one hand and on the other hand praying non-verbally through the spirit: 'For if I pray in a tongue, my spirit prays, but my mind is unfruitful. So what shall I do? I will pray with my spirit, but I will also pray with my mind; I will sing with my spirit, but I will also sing with my mind' (1 Corinthians 14:15).

Please send prayer room artwork for the 24–7 gallery to info@24-7prayer.com (JPEG or GIF file).

'In this room, I have had the freedom to express my love to God through art. Paint is magic - so is God.'
(Abi)

RESOURCES

(THE REALLY USEFUL BITS)

24-7 prayer and
Youth With A Mission
BY LYNN GREEN
(VICE PRESIDENT, YWAM)

I was a student in a Youth With A Mission Training School in 1970, when a New Zealander housewife named Joy Dawson came to teach for a month. She taught an uncompromising message of 'Knowing God' and being committed to intercessory prayer. Some of the prayer meetings that ensued were super-exciting. We realised that we were 'creating with God', and that God himself had given us the opportunity to participate in something that was important for his kingdom.

In one all night prayer meeting, I was part of a team in Afghanistan that was battling against the chaos and despair we had found in lives of young people who had travelled East to find spiritual reality. So many seemed to become demonised during the course of their contact with various religious groups in India and points East. Because we were trying to help people who were suicidal or dying of dysentery, or suffering from deep mental illness, our prayers were fervent that night and sleepiness was not a problem.

At about 5 o'clock in the morning, Manfred, a young German who had been suicidal for days, walked into our prayer room uninvited and unannounced and sat down in the middle of the team. As we prayed for him, he was delivered and restored to his right mind. He never again tried to commit suicide.

I can't claim that all our prayer meetings were that exciting, nor were they always so immediately effective. But I can claim that God has consistently spoken to us and broken into our world through regular and sacrificial prayer. Some of those prayer times have been long and hard, and often I have battled to stay awake.

Today, some 30 years later, YWAM consists of over 10,000 people – not 50 or 60 full-timers as at the beginning of 1970. This movement is built on prayer, and I would imagine that there have now been millions of hours of prayer meetings in every nation of the world, and by tens of thousands of people.

This life of prayer can only be sustained through regular injections of inspiration and new life. 24-7 represents one of those injections, and I for one stand in need of it. No doubt all of YWAM will welcome the zeal and inspiration of 24-7. We also welcome the new life that God is pouring out around the world in other parts of the body of Christ. Once again, God is bringing 'fresh streams in the desert' through an unexpected and unlikely (and therefore typical of God) movement.

24-7 prayer and the Salvation Army

BY COMMISSIONER ALEX HUGHES
(TERRITORIAL COMMANDER,
UK & NORTHERN IRELAND)

Hundreds of Salvation Army churches across the UK have done 24–7 prayer weeks, and have grown and changed as a result. But 24–7 prayer has had an even wider impact on the mission of our movement.

Lawley House is a hostel for men in Bradford, and in December 2001, the staff and residents held a week of 24–7 prayer. The hostel takes in men who are homeless, and often have an addiction of some kind. Most of the residents are not Christians. No one was quite sure how well a week of prayer would be received.

They began with a prayer concert, at which the Bishop of Bradford knelt and prayed with some of the homeless men. It was a powerful reminder of the open access God offers us in prayer, regardless of background or religious credentials. As the week went on, the staff and residents (Christian and non-Christian alike) spent hours and hours in the prayer room, enjoying God and pouring out their hearts to him. Many of the men met God for the first time in their lives.

24–7 prayer has helped us recapture something of the fire and passion of those early Salvation Army leaders who didn't make any distinction between prayer and physical care – they simply met people's needs. They knew that people needed to encounter the living God just as urgently as they needed bread and shelter, so they went for the truly holistic approach and prayed them into the kingdom while serving them a decent meal.

I had the privilege of being present at ROOTS when 24–7 prayer was launched at Christchurch in Southport. At that point we had no idea what God was going to do through this challenge. It has been an incredible journey and God has come to us in such marvellous ways. He has shown us more and more what it means to depend on him.

It has been my privilege to encourage many people to take up the challenge of 24–7 prayer and we have seen it happen not only in Salvation Army centres, but also together with other churches. It presents wonderful opportunities of being creative in prayer, but above all we have begun to relearn what it means to have prayer at the centre of our mission and mission at the centre of our prayer.

I think 24–7 prayer is one of the greatest things we have experienced in recent years and we will never be the same again.

24-7 vision and values

As an international prayer movement 24–7 unites around its vision and values rather than any particular structure, and these are expressed differently in every culture. We will work with anyone who shares this heartbeat. What's more, because we're committed to being relational, we gather every year at our Round Table to ensure that our vision is still true to our relationships and the call that God has put upon us together. To understand 24–7, simply explore our vision and values, which are currently as follows:

> **Vision**
>
> '24–7 prayer exists to transform the world through a movement of Christ-centred and mission-minded prayer.'

Values

Obedient to the Holy Spirit

Like Jesus, we seek to do what we see the Father doing. We acknowledge his right to break our rules and offend our sensibilities (John 5:19; Psalm 127:1; John 3:8).

Relational

We are a community of friends with shared vision and values, driven by friendship rather than function (John 15:14–15; Luke 10:1–22; 1 Peter 4:7–11; 1 John 4:7–12).

Indigenous

We respect, value and honour cultural diversity (Revelation 7:9–10; Daniel 1; 1 Corinthians 9:20–21).

Inclusive

We work with anyone sharing our vision and values, regardless of race, age, gender or church background. We build unity and enjoy diversity (Colossians 3:11; Ephesians 4:3–6).

Like Jesus

We seek to be like Jesus in the way we do what we do. For us, the means do not necessarily justify the ends.

Deep rooted

We are committed to growth in maturity rather than size (Psalm 1:1–3).

Creative and innovative

We embrace God-inspired creativity as integral to authentic expressions of prayer (Exodus 35:30–35; Genesis 1:1–2; Psalm 45:1; Proverbs 8:22–31).

Just

We will pursue justice and freedom from oppression for humanity and the created world (Isaiah 61; Luke 4:18–19; Romans 8:19–21; Isaiah 58).

Good stewards

We take responsibility for ourselves, those around us and the things that God has entrusted to us (Matthew 25:14–30; 2 Corinthians 9:6–15).

Sacrificial

We believe that a lifestyle of prayer is costly at every level (2 Corinthians 8:1–5; 1 John 3:16–18; Romans 12:1–2).

Celebratory

We believe that Jesus came to bring life to the full and that we have a Christian duty to celebrate all that is good. Fun and laughter are central to 24–7 and we do not need to justify these (Genesis 1:31; Psalm 24:1; Matthew 11:19; John 10:10).

Raw/simple

We are a network of like-minded people, not some new

slick organisation. In character we are wild and unpolished – passionate about developing people rather than our own profile (Psalm 116:6; Luke 10:3–5; John 3:8).

Resources available

WOW – 'I have posted **W**atchmen **O**n your **W**alls, O Jerusalem; they will never be silent day or night' (Isaiah 62:6). WOW is our SMS text messaging service which sends prayer alerts and Bible texts direct to your mobile phone. Visit www.24-7wow.com <http://www.24-7wow.com> to get connected.

PLAY TO PRAY – At 24–7 everything we do comes back to prayer. We produce CDs designed to help you go deeper with God. More than anything we want to help you make history, by praying and obeying like never before. Currently available:

- 24–7 ROCK
- 24–7 CHILL CD
- 24–7 BREAKS & BEATS
- 24–7 WORSHIP

START-UP PACK – This pack is jammed with cell notes, 60-minute prayer guides and much more to help you prepare for your first 24–7 prayer room.

T-SHIRTS/HOODIES – Get the T-shirt (wear the prayer!)

DOG TAGS – Produced in the factory that supplies the US military but with prayer words inscribed.

All available from 24-7prayer.com/shop

PS: Look out for two new books on 24-7 in 2004 - *Red Moon Rising* and *The Vision*.

24-7 disclaimer

With hundreds of prayer rooms all over the world, 24-7prayer.com cannot accept responsibility for anything that does or does not take place in these venues or in relation to their use. We urge bodies organising prayer rooms to ensure that proper safety procedures are implemented for each prayer room and its users. In registering a prayer room with 24–7 you accept full liability for the building used for 24–7 prayer and for the safety of those using the facility in relation to 24–7 prayer.

If you have any enquiries about safety and security not covered in the *24–7 Prayer Manual*, please don't hesitate to contact your nearest base. 24-7prayer.com is an umbrella organisation and does not control, and therefore accepts no liability for, the contents of participants' websites, who have been advised to take care to abide by the laws of their host nation.

(24–7 Prayer is a registered charity no. 1091413)

Useful contacts
24-7 OFFICES AND BASES

Australian base
24–7 Australia
PO Box 8070
Tumbi Umbi
New South Wales
2261
Australia
0061 2 4389 8151
australia@24-7prayer.com
www.24-7prayer.com/australia

Canadian office
24–7 Canada
561 Costigan Rd
Saskatoon
SK
S7J 3P9
Canada
0030 6 262 1071

Canada@24-7prayer.com
www.24-7prayer.com/canada

German base
24–7 Germany
Alaunstrasse 30
01099
Dresden
Germany
0049 351 810 8892
germany@24-7prayer.com
www.24-7prayer.com/germany

Indonesian office
Indonesia@24-7prayer.com

Japanese office
24–7 Japan
4–14–305 Koshikiwa–cho
Nishinomiya City
662 0092
Japan
0081 798 71 7331
japan@24-7prayer.com
www.24-7prayer.com/japan

Mexican office
24–7 Mexico
Bahia de Altata #1855
Col. Nvo. Culiacan CP 80170

Culiacan
Sinaloa
Mexico
0052 667 714 1566
mexico@24-7prayer.com
www.24-7prayer.com/spain

Spanish-speaking base
24–7 Spain
Apartodo 40–42
Seville
40180
Spain
0034 95 437 1191
spain@24-7prayer.com
www.24-7prayer.com/spain

Swedish base
24–7 Sweden
PO Box 1624
S–701 16 Orebro
Sweden
0046 19 167 682
Sweden@24-7prayer.com
www.24-7prayer.com/sweden

US office
24–7 USA
USA@24-7prayer.com

UK and international base
24–7 UK
PO Box 58
Chichester
West Sussex
PO19 8UD
UK
0044 1243 531 898 x 2
info@24-7prayer.com
www.24-7prayer.com

Useful websites
Prayer Rooms: www.24-7prayer.com
Mission Teams: www.24-7mission.com
Boiler Rooms: www.boiler-rooms.com
Operation World: www.24-7prayer.com/ow
Chat Forums: www.24-7talkback.com
SMS Text Messaging Service (UK only):
    www.24-7prayer.com/wow

**Prayer Room Support Helpline (UK): + 44 (0) 8710
97 11 99**

Notes

1. Brian and Kevin Draper, *Refreshing Worship* (Bible Reading Fellowship, 2000), p. 25.
2. Jack Hayford, *Worship His Majesty* (Paternoster, 1987). Cited in *Spring Harvest Study Guide 2003* by Gerard Kelly.
3. C. T. R. Hayward, *The Jewish Temple – A Non-Biblical Sourcebook* (Routledge, 1996), p. 23.
4. R. Taft, *The Liturgy of the Hours in East and West* (Minnesota: The Liturgical Press, 1986).
5. *Ibid.*, p. 15.
6. *Ibid.*, pp. 165–86.
7. Daniel Caner, *Wandering, Begging Monks – Spiritual Authority and the Promotion of Monasticism in Late Antiquity* (Los Angeles: University of California Press, 2002), p. 142.
8. http://pharos.bu.edu./cn/Menu.html
9. John Wesley's Journal.
10. Jenny Roberts, *Windows to Eternity* (Bible Reading Fellowship, 1999), p. 57.

11. Alvin J. Vander Griend, *The Praying Church Source Book* (Grand Rapids, MI: CRC Publications, 1997).

12. R. Taft, *op cit.*, pp. 68–9.

13. Alvin J. Vander Griend, *op cit.*, p. 194.

14. Terence E. Fretheim, *Interpretation: Exodus*, pp. 269–70.

Other Survivor books include . . .

The Unquenchable Worshipper
by Matt Redman

This book is about a kind of worshipper.
Unquenchable. Undivided. Unpredictable.
On a quest to bring glory and pleasure to
God, these worshippers will not allow
themselves to be distracted or defeated.
They long for their hearts, lives and songs to
be the kind of offerings God is looking for.

*'This is unashamedly a book about God and
living a devoted life in His presence. Worship is
about God, to God and for God.* The
Unquenchable Worshipper *shouts this truth
out loud.'* (Mike Pilavachi, Soul Survivor)

Wasteland?
by Mike Pilavachi

Are you looking for greater depth in your
Christian life? Tired of the consumer model
of spirituality? Are you ready to do the *right*
things, even when things are going *wrong*?
Feel like investing in obscurity . . . ?
Mountain tops can be invigorating, but
there's growth in the valleys. God says,
'Meet me in the desert.'

*'Mike Pilavachi draws on his own experience
and the Bible to infuse faith, hope and love in
us, and to inspire us on our journey.'*
(J. John, Philo Trust)

survivor